THE WISDOM
OF CONFUCIUS

ART-TYPE EDITION

THE WISDOM OF CONFUCIUS

With critical and biographical sketches by
EPIPHANIUS WILSON, A.M.

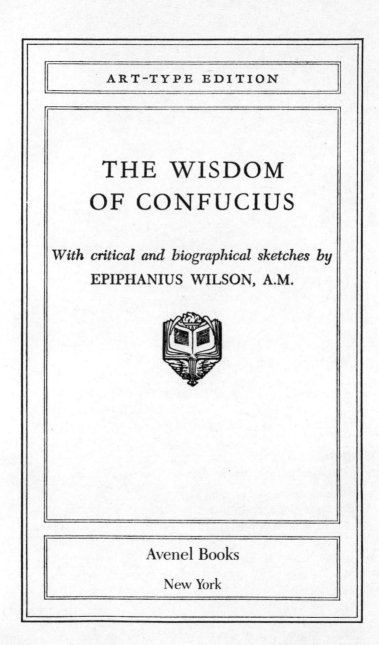

Avenel Books

New York

This 1982 edition is published by Avenel Books,
distributed by Crown Publishers, Inc.

Manufactured in the United States of America

Library of Congress Cataloging in Publication Data

Confucius.
    The wisdom of Confucius.

    Selected translation of: Lun yü.
    Reprint. Originally published: New York: Books, Inc.,
1900. (The world's popular classics)
    I. Jennings, William, 1847-1927.   II. Wilson, Epiphan-
ius, 1845-1916.   III. Title.   IV. Series: World's popular
classics.
PL2478.L4 1982   181'.09512   82-3919
ISBN 0-517-381060   AACR2
g f e d c b

CONTENTS

THE WISDOM OF CONFUCIUS

PAGE

Foreword xi

Introduction 3

BOOK

    I. On Learning—Miscellaneous Sayings 8

    II. Good Government—Filial Piety—The Superior Man 12

    III. Abuse of Proprieties in Ceremonial and Music . 16

    IV. Social Virtue—Superior and Inferior Man . . . 22

    V. A Disciple and the Golden Rule—Miscellaneous 25

    VI. More Characteristics—Wisdom—Philanthropy . . 31

    VII. Characteristics of Confucius—An Incident . . 36

    VIII. Sayings of Tsang—Sentences of the Master . . 42

    IX. His Favorite Disciple's Opinion of Him 46

    X. Confucius in Private and Official Life 51

    XI. Comparative Worth of His Disciples 56

    XII. The Master's Answers—Philanthropy—Friendships 62

    XIII. Answers on the Art of Governing—Consistency . 68

    XIV. Good and Bad Government—Miscellaneous Sayings 75

    XV. Practical Wisdom—Reciprocity the Rule of Life . 83

    XVI. Against Intestine Strife—Good and Bad Friendships 88

    XVII. The Master Induced to Take Office—Nature and Habit 93

    XVIII. Good Men in Seclusion—Duke of Chow to His Son 99

    XIX. Teachings of Various Chief Disciples 103

    XX. Extracts from the Book of History 108

THE SAYINGS OF MENCIUS

Introduction 113

BOOK I. King Hwuy of Lëang.

    Part I. 115

v

[*Books II, III, and IV are omitted*]

PAGE

BOOK V. Wan Chang.
Part I. 128

THE SHI-KING

Introduction 143

Part I. Lessons from the States.

BOOK I. THE ODES OF CHOW AND THE SOUTH.
Celebrating the Virtue of King Wan's Bride . . . 145
Celebrating the Industry of King Wan's Queen . . 146
In Praise of a Bride 146
Celebrating T'ae-Sze's Freedom from Jealousy . . 147
The Fruitfulness of the Locust 147
Lamenting the Absence of a Cherished Friend . . 148
Celebrating the Goodness of the Descendants of King
Wan 149
The Virtuous Manners of the Young Women . . . 149
Praise of a Rabbit-Catcher 150
The Song of the Plantain-Gatherers 151
The Affection of the Wives on the Joo 151
BOOK II. THE ODES OF SHAOU AND THE SOUTH.
The Marriage of a Princess 152
The Industry and Reverence of a Prince's Wife . . 152
The Wife of Some Great Officer Bewails his Absence . 153
The Diligence of the Young Wife of an Officer . . 154
The Love of the People for the Duke of Shaou . . 154
The Easy Dignity of the Officers at Some Court . . 155
Anxiety of a Young Lady to Get Married 155
BOOK III. THE ODES OF P'EI.
An Officer Bewails the Neglect with which He is
Treated 157
A Wife Deplores the Absence of Her Husband . . 158
The Plaint of a Rejected Wife 159
Soldiers of Wei Bewail Separation from their Families 161
An Officer Tells of His Mean Employment . . . 161
An Officer Sets Forth His Hard Lot 162

PAGE

The Complaint of a Neglected Wife 163
In Praise of a Maiden 164
Discontent 164
Chwang Keang Bemoans Her Husband's Cruelty . 165

[*Books IV, V, and VI are omitted*]

BOOK VII. THE ODES OF CH'ING.
    The People's Admiration for Duke Woo 167
    A Wife Consoled by Her Husband's Arrival . . . 168
    In Praise of Some Lady 168
    A Man's Praise of His Wife 169
    An Entreaty 169
    A Woman Scorning Her Lover 169
    A Lady Mourns the Absence of Her Student Lover . 170
BOOK VIII. THE ODES OF TS'E.
    A Wife Urging Her Husband to Action 171
    The Folly of Useless Effort 172
    The Prince of Loo 172
BOOK IX. THE ODES OF WEI.
    On the Misgovernment of the State 174
    The Mean Husband 175
    A Young Soldier on Service 175
BOOK X. THE ODES OF T'ANG.
    The King Goes to War 177
    Lament of a Bereaved Person 178
    The Drawbacks of Poverty 179
    A Wife Mourns for Her Husband 179
BOOK XI. THE ODES OF TS'IN.
    Celebrating the Opulence of the Lords of Ts'in . . 181
    A Complaint 182
    A Wife's Grief Because of Her Husband's Absence . 182
    Lament for Three Brothers 183
    In Praise of a Ruler of Ts'in 184
    The Generous Nephew 185
BOOK XII. THE ODES OF CH'IN.
    The Contentment of a Poor Recluse 186
    The Disappointed Lover 186

PAGE

A Love-Song 187
The Lament of a Lover 187
BOOK XIII. THE ODES OF KWEI.
The Wish of an Unhappy Man 189
BOOK XIV. THE ODES OF TS'AOU.
Against Frivolous Pursuits 190
BOOK XV. THE ODES OF PIN.
The Duke of Chow Tells of His Soldiers 191
There is a Proper Way for Doing Everything . . . 192

Part II. Minor Odes of the Kingdom.

BOOK I. DECADE OF LUH MING.
A Festal Ode 194
A Festal Ode Complimenting an Officer 195
The Value of Friendship 196
The Response to a Festal Ode 198
An Ode of Congratulation 199
An Ode on the Return of the Troops 200
BOOK II. THE DECADE OF PIH HWA.
An Ode Appropriate to a Festivity 203
BOOK III. THE DECADE OF T'UNG KUNG.
Celebrating a Hunting Expedition 204
The King's Anxiety for His Morning Levee . . . 205
Moral Lessons from Natural Facts 206
BOOK IV. THE DECADE OF K'E-FOO.
On the Completion of a Royal Palace 207
The Cnodition of King Seuen's Flocks 208
BOOK V. THE DECADE OF SEAOU MIN.
A Eunuch Complains of His Fate 210
An Officer Deplores the Misery of the Time . . . 212
On the Alienation of a Friend 213
BOOK VI. THE DECADE OF PIH SHAN.
A Picture of Husbandry 215
The Complaint of an Officer 216
BOOK VII. DECADE OF SANG HOO.
The Rejoicings of a Bridegroom 219
Against Listening to Slanderers 220

PAGE

BOOK VIII. THE DECADE OF TOO JIN SZE.
    In Praise of By-gone Simplicity 221
    A Wife Bemoans Her Husband's Absence 222
    The Earl of Shaou's Work 223
    The Plaint of King Yew's Forsaken Wife 224
    Hospitality 226
    On the Misery of Soldiers 226

Part III. Greater Odes of the Kingdom.

BOOK I. DECADE OF KING WAN.
    Celebrating King Wan 228

[Book II is omitted]

BOOK III. DECADE OF TANG.
    King Seuen on the Occasion of a Great Drought . . 231

Part IV. Odes of the Temple and Altar.

BOOK I. SACRIFICIAL ODES OF CHOW.
    Appropriate to a Sacrifice to King Wan 235
    On Sacrificing to the Kings Woo, Ching, and K'ang . 236

FOREWORD

Confucius, born in 550 B.C., remains a major influence on Chinese thought and culture. The principles and concepts that he taught his followers are an integral part of the Chinese character of today.

Confucianism has as one of its major tenets a version of the golden rule that states, "What you do not want done to yourself do not do to others." This belief transferred to western culture as, "Do unto others as you would have them do unto you." Confucius was concerned with man's actions on earth, not with what would happen to a man after death, or with the metaphysical question of whether he would be punished or rewarded for his actions on earth. None of his teachings deals with the concept of an afterlife, only with how one should live—"While you do not know life, what can you know about death?" It was by following his golden rule that Confucius believed one could live a good life.

Convinced that man was basically good, Confucius felt people were led by example—a model ruler would be assured of a model populace. The emperor was appointed by heaven to serve as a father and mother to the country, and it was his responsibility to lead his people by example. Confucius believed that, "Not more surely does the grass bend before the wind than the masses yield to the will of those above them."

Besides the ruler-subject relationship, Confucius outlined four others: husband-wife, father-son, older brother-younger brother, and friend-friend. These relationships are based on the reciprocity expressed in the afore-mentioned golden rule: "What you do not want done to yourself do not do to others." In all these relationships there is a person who is dominant and one who is submissive, yet both are striving for virtue and the dominant member in a benevolent manner is showing the way for the submissive member.

Confucius also outlined five primary virtues—love, justice, reverence, wisdom, and sincerity. These virtues are the guideposts for man's actions. Many of Confucius' sayings—"What the superior man seeks is in himself; what the small man seeks is in others" or "The cautious seldom err"—reflect these virtues.

The Wisdom of Confucius is a compilation of the sayings of Confucius and his disciple Mencius, who devoted his life to spreading the teachings of Confucius. Even though Confucius lived well over two thousand years ago, his sayings are still fresh, thoughtful, and meaningful for modern readers.

A. JAMES FICKLEN

THE WISDOM
OF CONFUCIUS

[Translated into English by William Jennings]

PRONUNCIATION OF PROPER NAMES

j, as in French.

ng, commencing a word, like the same letters terminating one.

ai or *ei*, as in *aisle* or *eider*.

au, as in German, or like *ow* in *cow*.

é, as in *fête*.

i (not followed by a consonant), as *ee* in *see*.

u (followed by a consonant), as in *bull.*

iu, as *ew* in *new*.

üi, as *ooi* in *cooing*.

h at the end of a name makes the preceding vowel short.

' in the middle of a word denotes an aspirate (h), as *K'ung = Khung*.

INTRODUCTION

THE strangest figure that meets us in the annals of Oriental thought is that of Confucius. To the popular mind he is the founder of a religion, and yet he has nothing in common with the great religious teachers of the East. We think of Siddartha, the founder of Buddhism, as the very impersonation of romantic asceticism, enthusiastic self-sacrifice, and faith in the things that are invisible. Zoroaster is the friend of God, talking face to face with the Almighty, and drinking wisdom and knowledge from the lips of Omniscience. Mohammed is represented as snatched up into heaven, where he receives the Divine communication which he is bidden to propagate with fire and sword throughout the world. These great teachers lived in an atmosphere of the supernatural. They spoke with the authority of inspired prophets. They brought the unseen world close to the minds of their disciples. They spoke positively of immortality, of reward or punishment beyond the grave. The present life they despised, the future was to them everything in its promised satisfaction. The teachings of Confucius were of a very different sort. Throughout his whole writings he has not even mentioned the name of God. He declined to discuss the question of immortality. When he was asked about spiritual beings, he remarked, "If we cannot even know men, how can we know spirits?"

Yet this was the man the impress of whose teaching has formed the national character of five hundred millions of people. A temple to Confucius stands to this day in every town and village of China. His precepts are committed to memory by every child from the tenderest age, and each year at the royal university at Pekin the Emperor holds a festival in honor of the illustrious teacher.

The influence of Confucius springs, first of all, from the narrowness and definiteness of his doctrine. He was no transcendentalist, and never meddled with supramundane things. His teaching was of the earth, earthy; it dealt entirely with the common relations of life, and the Golden Rule he must necessarily have stumbled upon, as the most obvious canon of his system. He strikes us as being the great Stoic of the East, for he believed that virtue was based on knowledge, knowledge of a man's own heart, and knowledge of human-kind. There is a pathetic resemblance between the accounts given of the death of Confucius and the death of Zeno. Both died almost without warning in dreary hopelessness, without the ministrations of either love or religion. This may be a mere coincidence, but the lives and teachings of both men must have led them to look with indifference upon such an end. For Confucius in his teaching treated only of man's life on earth, and seems to have had no ideas with regard to the human lot after death; if he had any ideas he preserved an inscrutable silence about them. As a moralist he prescribed the duties of the king and of the father, and advocated the cultivation by the individual man of that rest or apathy of mind which resembles so much the disposition aimed at by the Greek and Roman Stoic. Even as a moralist, he seems to have sacrificed the ideal to the practical, and his loose notions about marriage, his tolerance of concubinage, the slight emphasis which he lays on the virtue of veracity—of which indeed he does not seem himself to have been particularly studious in his historic writings—place him low down in the rank of moralists. Yet he taught what he felt the people could receive, and the flat mediocrity of his character and his teachings has been stamped forever upon a people who, while they are kindly, gentle, forbearing, and full of family piety, are palpably lacking not only in the exaltation of Mysticism, but in any religious feeling, generally so-called.

The second reason that made the teaching of Confucius so influential is based on the circumstances of the time. When this thoughtful, earnest youth awoke to the consciousness of life about him, he saw that the abuses under which the people groaned sprang from the feudal system, which cut up the country into separate territories, over which the power of the king had no control. China was in the position of France in the years preceding Philippe-Auguste, excepting that there were no places of sanctuary and no Truce of God. The great doctrine of Confucius was the unlimited despotism of the Emperor, and his moral precepts were intended to teach the Emperor how to use his power aright. But the Emperor was only typical of all those in authority—the feudal duke, the judge on the bench, and the father of the family. Each could discharge his duties aright only by submitting to the moral discipline which Confucius prescribed. A vital element in this system is its conservatism, its adherence to the imperial idea. As James I said, "No bishop, no king," so the imperialists of China have found in Confucianism the strongest basis for the throne, and have supported its dissemination accordingly.

The Analects of Confucius contain the gist of his teachings, and is worthy of study. We find in this work most of the precepts which his disciples have preserved and recorded. They form a code remarkable for simplicity, even crudity, and we are compelled to admire the force of character, the practical sagacity, the insight into the needs of the hour, which enabled Confucius, without claiming any Divine sanction, to impose this system upon his country-men.

The name Confucius is only the Latinized form of two words which mean "Master K'ung." He was born 551 B.C., his father being governor of Shantung. He was married at nineteen, and seems to have occupied some minor position under the government. In his twenty-fourth year he entered upon the three years' mourning for the death of his mother. His seclusion gave him time for deep thought and the study of history, and he resolved upon the regeneration of his unhappy country. By the time he was thirty he became known as a great teacher, and disciples flocked to him. But he was yet occupied in public duties, and rose through successive stages to the office of Chief Judge in his own country of Lu. His tenure of office is said to have put an end to crime, and he became the "idol of the people" in his district. The jealousy of the feudal lords was roused by his fame as a moral teacher and a blameless judge. Confucius was driven from his home, and wandered about, with a few disciples, until his sixty-ninth year, when he returned to Lu, after accomplishing a work which has borne fruit, such as it is, to the present day. He spent the remaining five years of his life in editing the odes and historic monuments in which the glories of the ancient Chinese dynasty are set forth. He died in his seventy-third year, 478 B.C. There can be no doubt that the success of Confucius has been singularly great, owing especially to the narrow scope of his scheme, which has become crystallized in the habits, usages, and customs of the people. Especially has it been instrumental in consolidating the empire, and in strengthening the power of the monarch, who, as he every year burns incense in the red-walled temple at Pekin, utters sincerely the invocation: "Great art thou, O perfect Sage! Thy virtue is full, thy doctrine complete.

Among mortal men there has not been thine equal. All kings honor thee. Thy statutes and laws have come gloriously down. Thou art the pattern in this imperial school. Reverently have the sacrificial vessels been set out. Full of awe, we sound our drums and bells."

E. W.

BOOK I

On Learning—Miscellaneous Sayings

"To learn," said the Master, "and then to practise opportunely what one has learnt—does not this bring with it a sense of satisfaction?

"To have associates in study coming to one from distant parts—does not this also mean pleasure in store?

"And are not those who, while not comprehending all that is said, still remain not unpleased to hear, men of the superior order?"

A saying of the Scholar Yu:—

"It is rarely the case that those who act the part of true men in regard to their duty to parents and elder brothers are at the same time willing to turn currishly upon their superiors: it has never yet been the case that such as desire not to commit that offence have been men willing to promote anarchy or disorder.

"Men of superior mind busy themselves first in getting at the root of things; and when they have succeeded in this the right course is open to them. Well, are not filial piety and friendly subordination among brothers a root of that right feeling which is owing generally from man to man?"

The Master observed, "Rarely do we meet with the right feeling due from one man to another where there is fine speech and studied mien."

The Scholar Tsang once said of himself: "On three points I examine myself daily, viz., whether, in looking after other people's interests, I have not been acting wholeheartedly; whether, in my intercourse with friends, I have not been true; and whether, after teaching, I have not my-self been practising what I have taught."

The Master once observed that to rule well one of the larger States meant strict attention to its affairs and con-scientiousness on the part of the ruler; careful husbanding of its resources, with at the same time a tender care for the interests of all classes; and the employing of the masses in the public service at suitable seasons.

"Let young people," said he, "show filial piety at home, respectfulness towards their elders when away from home; let them be circumspect, be truthful; their love going out freely towards all, cultivating good-will to men. And if, in such a walk, there be time or energy left for other things, let them employ it in the acquisition of literary or artistic accomplishments."

The disciple Tsz-hiá said, "The appreciation of worth in men of worth, thus diverting the mind from lascivious de-sires—ministering to parents while one is the most capable of so doing—serving one's ruler when one is able to devote himself entirely to that object—being sincere in one's lan-guage in intercourse with friends: this I certainly must call evidence of learning, though others may say there has been 'no learning.' "

Sayings of the Master:—

"If the great man be not grave, he will not be revered, neither can his learning be solid.

"Give prominent place to loyalty and sincerity.

"Have no associates in study who are not advanced somewhat like yourself.

"When you have erred, be not afraid to correct your-self."

A saying of the Scholar Tsang:—

"The virtue of the people is renewed and enriched when attention is seen to be paid to the departed, and the re-membrance of distant ancestors kept and cherished."

Tsz-k'in put this query to his fellow disciple Tsz-kung: said he, "When our Master comes to this or that State, he learns without fail how it is being governed. Does he investigate matters? or are the facts given him?"

Tsz-kung answered, "Our Master is a man of pleasant manners, and of probity, courteous, moderate, and unassuming: it is by his being such that he arrives at the facts. Is not his way of arriving at things different from that of others?"

A saying of the Master:—

"He who, after three years' observation of the will of his father when alive, or of his past conduct if dead, does not deviate from that father's ways, is entitled to be called 'a dutiful son.'"

Sayings of the Scholar Yu:—

"For the practice of the Rules of Propriety,[1] one excellent way is to be natural. This naturalness became a great grace in the practice of kings of former times; let everyone, small or great, follow their example.

"It is not, however, always practicable; and it is not so in the case of a person who does things naturally, knowing that he should act so, and yet who neglects to regulate his acts according to the Rules.

"When truth and right are hand in hand, a statement will bear repetition. When respectfulness and propriety go hand in hand, disgrace and shame are kept afar-off. Remove all occasion for alienating those to whom you are bound by close ties, and you have them still to resort to."

A saying of the Master:—

"The man of greater mind who, when he is eating, craves not to eat to the full; who has a home, but craves not for comforts in it; who is active and earnest in his work and

[1] An important part of a Chinaman's education still. The text-book, "The Li Ki," contains rules for behavior and propriety for the whole life, from the cradle to the grave.

careful in his words; who makes towards men of high principle, and so maintains his own rectitude—that man may be styled a devoted student."

Tsz-kung asked, "What say you, sir, of the poor who do not cringe and fawn; and what of the rich who are without pride and haughtiness?" "They are passable," the Master replied; "yet they are scarcely in the same category as the poor who are happy, and the rich who love propriety."

"In the 'Book of the Odes,'" Tsz-kung went on to say, "we read of one

> Polished, as by the knife and file,
> The graving-tool, the smoothing-stone.

Does that coincide with your remark?"

"Ah! such as you," replied the Master, "may well commence a discussion on the Odes. If one tell you how a thing goes, you know what ought to come."

"It does not greatly concern me," said the Master, "that men do not know me; my great concern is, my not knowing them."

BOOK II

Good Government—Filial Piety—The Superior Man

SAYINGS of the Master:—

"Let a ruler base his government upon virtuous principles, and he will be like the pole-star, which remains steadfast in its place, while all the host of stars turn towards it.

"The 'Book of Odes' contains three hundred pieces, but one expression in it may be taken as covering the purport of all, viz., Unswerving mindfulness.

"To govern simply by statute, and to reduce all to order by means of pains and penalties, is to render the people evasive, and devoid of any sense of shame.

"To govern upon principles of virtue, and to reduce them to order by the Rules of Propriety, would not only create in them the sense of shame, but would moreover reach them in all their errors.

"When I attained the age of fifteen, I became bent upon study. At thirty, I was a confirmed student. At forty, nought could move me from my course. At fifty, I comprehended the will and decrees of Heaven. At sixty, my ears were attuned to them. At seventy, I could follow my heart's desires, without overstepping the lines of rectitude."

To a question of Mang-i, as to what filial piety consisted in, the Master replied, "In not being perverse." Afterwards, when Fan Ch'i was driving him, the Master informed him of this question and answer, and Fan Ch'i asked, "What was your meaning?" The Master replied, "I meant that the Rules of Propriety should always be adhered to in regard to those who brought us into the world: in ministering to them while living, in burying them when dead, and afterwards in the offering to them of sacrificial gifts."

To a query of Mang Wu respecting filial piety, the Master replied, "Parents ought to bear but one trouble—that of their own sickness."

To a like question put by Tsz-yu, his reply was this: "The filial piety of the present day simply means the being able to support one's parents—which extends even to the case of dogs and horses, all of which may have something to give in the way of support. If there be no reverential feeling in the matter, what is there to distinguish between the cases?"

To a like question of Tsz-hiá, he replied: "The manner is the difficulty. If, in the case of work to be done, the younger folks simply take upon themselves the toil of it; or if, in the matter of meat and drink, they simply set these before their elders—is this to be taken as filial piety?"

Once the Master remarked, "I have conversed with Hwúi the whole day long, and he has controverted nothing that I have said, as if he were without wits. But when his back was turned, and I looked attentively at his conduct apart from me, I found it satisfactory in all its issues. No, indeed! Hwúi is not without his wits."

Other observations of the Master:—

"If you observe what things people (usually) take in hand, watch their motives, and note particularly what it is that gives them satisfaction, shall they be able to conceal from you what they are? Conceal themselves, indeed!

"Be versed in ancient lore, and familiarize yourself with the modern; then may you become teachers.

"The great man is not a mere receptacle."

In reply to Tsz-kung respecting the great man:—

"What he first says, as a result of his experience, he afterwards follows up.

"The great man is catholic-minded, and not one-sided. The common man is the reverse.

"Learning, without thought, is a snare; thought, without learning, is a danger.

"Where the mind is set much upon heterodox principles —there truly and indeed is harm."

To the disciple of Tsz-lu the Master said, "Shall I give you a lesson about knowledge? When you know a thing, maintain that you know it; and when you do not, acknowledge your ignorance. This is characteristic of knowledge."

Tsz-chang was studying with an eye to official income. The Master addressed him thus: "Of the many things you hear hold aloof from those that are doubtful, and speak guardedly with reference to the rest; your mistakes will then be few. Also, of the many courses you see adopted, hold aloof from those that are risky, and carefully follow the others; you will then seldom have occasion for regret. Thus, being seldom mistaken in your utterances, and having few occasions for regret in the line you take, you are on the high road to your preferment."

To a question put to him by Duke Ngai[1] as to what should be done in order to render the people submissive to authority, Confucius replied, "Promote the straightforward, and reject those whose courses are crooked, and the thing will be effected. Promote the crooked and reject the straightforward, and the effect will be the reverse."

When Ki K'ang[2] asked of him how the people could be induced to show respect, loyalty, and willingness to be led, the Master answered, "Let there be grave dignity in him who has the oversight of them, and they will show him respect; let him be seen to be good to his own parents, and

[1] Of Lu (Confucius's native State).
[2] Head of one of the "Three Families" of Lu.

kindly in disposition, and they will be loyal to him; let him promote those who have ability, and see to the instruction of those who have it not, and they will be willing to be led."

Some one, speaking to Confucius, inquired, "Why, sir, are you not an administrator of government?" The Master rejoined, "What says the 'Book of the Annals,' with reference to filial duty?—'Make it a point to be dutiful to your parents and amicable with your brethren; the same duties extend to an administrator.' If these, then, also make an administrator, how am I to take your words about being an administrator?"

On one occasion the Master remarked, "I know not what men are good for, on whose word no reliance can be placed. How should your carriages, large or little, get along without your whipple-trees or swing-trees?"

Tsz-chang asked if it were possible to forecast the state of the country ten generations hence. The Master replied in this manner: "The Yin dynasty adopted the rules and manners of the Hiá line of kings, and it is possible to tell whether it retrograded or advanced. The Chow line has followed the Yin, adopting its ways, and whether there has been deterioration or improvement may also be determined. Some other line may take up in turn those of Chow; and supposing even this process to go on for a hundred generations, the result may be known."

Other sayings of the Master:—

"It is but flattery to make sacrificial offerings to departed spirits not belonging to one's own family.

"It is moral cowardice to leave undone what one perceives to be right to do."

BOOK III

Abuse of Proprieties in Ceremonial and Music

ALLUDING to the head of the Ki family,[1] and the eight lines of posturers[2] before their ancestral hall, Confucius remarked, "If the Ki can allow himself to go to this extent, to what extent will he not allow himself to go?"

The Three Families[3] were in the habit, during the Removal of the sacred vessels after sacrifice, of using the hymn commencing

> "Harmoniously the Princes
> Draw near with reverent tread,
> Assisting in his worship
> Heaven's Son, the great and dread."

"How," exclaimed the Master, "can such words be appropriated i nthe ancestral hall of the Thre Families?"

"Where a man," said he again, "has not the proper feelings due from one man to another, how will he stand as regards the Rules of Propriety? And in such a case, what shall we say of his sense of harmony?"

[1] The Chief of the Ki clan was virtually the Duke of Lu, under whom Confucius for a time held office.

[2] These posturers were mutes who took part in the ritual of the ancestral temple, waving plumes, flags, etc. Each line or rank of these contained eight men. Only in the sovereign's household should there have been eight lines of them; a ducal family like the Ki should have had but six lines; a great official had four, and one of lower grade two. These were the gradations marking the status of families, and Confucius's sense of propriety was offended at the Ki's usurping in this way the appearance of royalty.

[3] Three great families related to each other, in whose hands the government of the State of Lu then was, and of which the Ki was the chief.

On a question being put to him by Lin Fang, a disciple, as to what was the radical idea upon which the Rules of Propriety were based, the Master exclaimed, "Ah! that is a large question. As to some rules, where there is likelihood of extravagance, they would rather demand economy; in those which relate to mourning, and where there is likelihood of being easily satisfied, what is wanted is real sorrow."

Speaking of the disorder of the times he remarked that while the barbarians on the North and East had their Chieftains, we here in this great country had nothing to compare with them in that respect:—we had lost these distinctions!

Alluding to the matter of the Chief of the Ki family worshipping on T'ai-shan,[4] the Master said to Yen Yu, "Cannot you save him from this?" He replied, "It is beyond my power." "Alas, alas!" exclaimed the Master, "are we to say that the spirits of T'ai-shan have not as much discernment as Lin Fang?"

Of "the superior man," the Master observed, "In him there is no contentiousness. Say even that he does certainly contend with others, as in archery competitions; yet mark, in that case, how courteously he will bow and go up for the forfeit-cup, and come down again and give it to his competitor. In his very contest he is still the superior man."

Tsz-hiá once inquired what inference might be drawn from the lines—

> "Dimples playing in witching smile,
> Beautiful eyes, so dark, so bright!
> Oh, and her face may be thought the while
> Colored by art, red rose on white!"

"Coloring," replied the Master, "requires a pure and clear background." "Then," said the other, "rules of ceremony

[4] One of the five sacred mountains, worshipped upon only by the sovereign.

require to have a background!" "Ah!" exclaimed the Master, "you are the man to catch the drift of my thought. Such as you may well introduce a discussion on the Odes."

Said the Master, "As regards the ceremonial adopted and enforced by the Hiá dynasty, I am able to describe it, although their own descendants in the State of Ki can adduce no adequate testimony in favor of its use there. So, too, I am able to describe the ceremonial of the Yin dynasty, although no more can the Sung people show sufficient reason for its continuance amongst themselves. And why cannot they do so? Because they have not documents enough, nor men learned enough. If only they had such, I could refer them to them in support of their usages.

"When I am present at the great quinquennial sacrifice to the *manes* of the royal ancestors," the Master said, "from the pouring-out of the oblation onwards, I have no heart to look on."

Some one asked what was the purport of this great sacrifice, and the Master replied, "I cannot tell. The position in the empire of him who could tell you is as evident as when you look at this"—pointing to the palm of his hand.

When he offered sacrifices to his ancestors, he used to act as if they were present before him. In offering to other spirits it was the same.

He would say, "If I do not myself take part in my offerings, it is all the same as if I did not offer them."

Wang-sun Kiá asked him once, "What says the proverb, 'Better to court favor in the kitchen than in the drawing-room'?" The Master replied, "Nay, better say, He who has sinned against Heaven has none other to whom prayer may be addressed."

Of the Chow dynasty the Master remarked, "It looks back upon two other dynasties; and what a rich possession it has in its records of those times! I follow Chow!"

On his first entry into the grand temple, he inquired

about every matter connected with its usages. Some one thereupon remarked, "Who says that the son of the man of Tsou⁵ understands about ceremonial? On entering the grand temple he inquired about everything." This remark coming to the Master's ears, he said, "What I did is part of the ceremonial!"

"In archery," he said, "the great point to be observed is not simply the perforation of the leather; for men have not all the same strength. That was the fashion in the olden days."

Once, seeing that his disciple Tsz-kung was desirous that the ceremonial observance of offering a sheep at the new moon might be dispensed with, the Master said, "Ah! you grudge the loss of the sheep; I grudge the loss of the ceremony."

"To serve one's ruler nowadays," he remarked, "fully complying with the Rules of Propriety, is regarded by others as toadyism!"

When Duke Ting questioned him as to how a prince should deal with his ministers, and how they in turn should serve their prince, Confucius said in reply, "In dealing with his ministers a prince should observe the proprieties; in serving his prince a minister should observe the duty of loyalty."

Referring to the First of the Odes, he remarked that it was mirthful without being lewd, and sad also without being painful.

Duke Ngai asked the disciple Tsai Wo respecting the places for sacrificing to the Earth. The latter replied, "The Family of the Great Yu, of the Hiá dynasty, chose a place of pine trees; the Yin founders chose cypresses; and the Chow founders chestnut trees, solemn and majestic, to inspire, 'tis said, the people with feelings of awe."

The Master on hearing of this exclaimed, "Never an allu-

⁵ Tsou was Confucius's birthplace; his father was governor of the town.

sion to things that have been enacted in the past! Never a remonstrance against what is now going on! He has gone away without a word of censure."

The Master once said of Kwan Chung,[6] "A small-minded man indeed!"

"Was he miserly?" some one asked.

"Miserly, indeed!" said he; "not that: he married three times, and he was not a man who restricted his official business to too few hands—how could he be miserly?"

"He knew the Rules of Propriety, I suppose?"

"Judge:—Seeing that the feudal lords planted a screen at their gates, he too would have one at his! Seeing that when any two of the feudal lords met in friendly conclave they had an earthenware stand on which to place their inverted cups after drinking, he must have the same! If he knew the Rules of Propriety, who is there that does not know them?"

In a discourse to the Chief Preceptor of Music at the court of Lu, the Master said, "Music is an intelligible thing. When you begin a performance, let all the various instruments produce as it were one sound (inharmonious); then, as you go on, bring out the harmony fully, distinctly, and with uninterrupted flow, unto the end."

The warden of the border-town of I requested an interview with Confucius, and said, "When great men have come here, I have never yet failed to obtain a sight of them." The followers introduced him; and, on leaving, he said to them, "Sirs, why grieve at his loss of office? The empire has for long been without good government; and Heaven is about to use your master as its edict-announcer."

Comparing the music of the emperor Shun with the mu-

---

[6] A renowned statesman who flourished about two hundred years before Confucius's time. A philosophical work on law and government, said to have been written by him, is still extant. He was regarded as a sage by the people, but he lacked, in Confucius's eyes, the one thing needful—propriety.

sic of King Wu, the Master said, "That of Shun is beautiful throughout, and also good throughout. That of Wu is all of it beautiful, but scarcely all of it good."

"High station," said the Master, "occupied by men who have no large and generous heart; ceremonial performed with no reverence; duties of mourning engaging the attention, where there is absence of sorrow;—how should I look on, where this is the state of things?"

BOOK IV

Social Virtue—Superior and Inferior Man

SAYINGS of the Master:—

"It is social good feeling that gives charm to a neighborhood. And where is the wisdom of those who choose an abode where it does not abide?

"Those who are without it cannot abide long, either in straitened or in happy circumstances. Those who possess it find contentment in it. Those who are wise go after it as men go after gain.

"Only they in whom it exists can have right likings and dislikings for others.

"Where the will is set upon it, there will be no room for malpractices.

"Riches and honor are what men desire; but if they arrive at them by improper ways, they should not continue to hold them. Poverty and low estate are what men dislike; but if they arrive at such a condition by improper ways, they should not refuse it.

"If the 'superior man' make nought of social good feeling, how shall he fully bear that name?

"Not even whilst he eats his meal will the 'superior man' forget what he owes to his fellow-men. Even in hurried leave-takings, even in moments of frantic confusion, he keeps true to this virtue.

"I have not yet seen a lover of philanthropy, nor a hater of misanthropy—such, that the former did not take occasion to magnify that virtue in himself, and that the latter, in his positive practice of philanthropy, did not, at times,

22

allow in his presence something savoring of misanthropy.

"Say you, is there any one who is able for one whole day to apply the energy of his mind to this virtue? Well, I have not seen any one whose energy was not equal to it. It may be there are such, but I have never met with them.

"The faults of individuals are peculiar to their particular class and surroundings; and it is by observing their faults that one comes to understand the condition of their good feelings towards their fellows.

"One may hear the right way in the morning, and at evening die.

"The scholar who is intent upon learning the right way, and who is yet ashamed of poor attire and poor food, is not worthy of being discoursed with.

"The masterly man's attitude to the world is not exclusively this or that: whatsoever is right, to that he will be a party.

"The masterly man has an eye to virtue, the common man, to earthly things; the former has an eye to penalties for error—the latter, to favor.

"Where there is habitual going after gain, there is much ill-will.

"When there is ability in a ruler to govern a country by adhering to the Rules of Propriety, and by kindly condescension, what is wanted more? Where the ability to govern thus is wanting, what has such a ruler to do with the Rules of Propriety?

"One should not be greatly concerned at not being in office; but rather about the requirements in one's self for such a standing. Neither should one be so much concerned at being unknown; but rather with seeking to become worthy of being known."

Addressing his disciple Tsang Sin, the Master said, "Tsang Sin, the principles which I inculcate have one main idea upon which they all hang." "Aye, surely," he replied.

When the Master was gone out the other disciples asked what was the purport of this remark. Tsang's answer was, "The principles of our Master's teaching are these—wholeheartedness and kindly forbearance; these and nothing more."

Other observations of the Master:—

"Men of loftier mind manifest themselves in their equitable dealings; small-minded men in their going after gain.

"When you meet with men of worth, think how you may attain to their level; when you see others of an opposite character, look within, and examine yourself.

"A son, in ministering to his parents, may (on occasion) offer gentle remonstrances; when he sees that their will is not to heed such, he should nevertheless still continue to show them reverent respect, never obstinacy; and if he have to suffer, let him do so without murmuring.

"Whilst the parents are still living, he should not wander far; or, if a wanderer, he should at least have some fixed address.

"If for three years he do not veer from the principles of his father, he may be called a dutiful son.

"A son should not ignore the years of his parents. On the one hand, they may be a matter for rejoicing (that they have been so many), and on the other, for apprehension (that so few remain).

"People in olden times were loth to speak out, fearing the disgrace of not being themselves as good as their words.

"Those who keep within restraints are seldom losers.

"To be slow to speak, but prompt to act, is the desire of the 'superior man.'

"Virtue dwells not alone: she must have neighbors."

An observation of Tsz-yu:—

"Officiousness, in the service of princes, leads to disgrace; among friends, to estrangement."

BOOK V

A *Disciple and the Golden Rule—Miscellaneous*

THE Master pronounced Kung-ye Ch'ang, a disciple, to be a marriageable person; for although lying bound in criminal fetters he had committed no crime. And he gave him his own daughter to wife.

Of Nan Yung, a disciple, he observed, that in a State where the government was well conducted he would not be passed over in its appointments, and in one where the government was ill conducted he would evade punishment and disgrace. And he caused his elder brother's daughter to be given in marriage to him.

Of Tsz-tsien, a disciple, he remarked, "A superior man indeed is the like of him! But had there been none of superior quality in Lu, how should this man have attained to this excellence?"

Tsz-kung asked, "What of me, then?" "You," replied the Master—"You are a receptacle." "Of what sort?" said he. "One for high and sacred use," was the answer.

Some one having observed of Yen Yung that he was good-natured towards others, but that he lacked the gift of ready speech, the Master said, "What need of that gift? To stand up before men and pour forth a stream of glib words is generally to make yourself obnoxious to them. I know not about his good-naturedness; but at any rate what need of that gift?"

When the Master proposed that Tsi-tiau K'ai should enter the government service, the latter replied, "I can scarcely credit it." The Master was gratified.

25

"Good principles are making no progress," once exclaimed the Master. "If I were to take a raft, and drift about on the sea, would Tsz-lu, I wonder, be my follower there?" That disciple was delighted at hearing the suggestion; whereupon the Master continued, "He surpasses me in his love of deeds of daring. But he does not in the least grasp the pith of my remark."

In reply to a question put to him by Mang Wu respecting Tsz-lu—as to whether he might be called good-natured towards others, the Master said, "I cannot tell"; but, on the question being put again, he answered, "Well, in an important State[1] he might be intrusted with the management of the military levies; but I cannot answer for his good nature."

"What say you then of Yen Yu?"

"As for Yen," he replied, "in a city of a thousand families, or in a secondary fief,[2] he might be charged with the governorship; but I cannot answer for his good-naturedness."

"Take Tsz-hwa, then; what of him?"

"Tsz-hwa," said he, "with a cincture girt upon him, standing as attendant at Court, might be charged with the addressing of visitors and guests; but as to his good-naturedness I cannot answer."

Addressing Tsz-kung, the Master said, "Which of the two is ahead of the other—yourself or Hwúi?" "How shall I dare," he replied, "even to look at Hwúi? Only let him hear one particular, and from that he knows ten; whereas I, if I hear one, may from it know two."

"You are not a match for him, I grant you," said the Master. "You are not his match."

Tsai Yu, a disciple, used to sleep in the daytime. Said the Master, "One may hardly carve rotten wood, or use a

---

[1] Lit., a State of 1,000 war chariots.
[2] Lit., a House of 100 war chariots.

trowel to the wall of a manure-yard! In his case, what is the use of reprimand?

"My attitude towards a man in my first dealings with him," he added, "was to listen to his professions and to trust to his conduct. My attitude now is to listen to his professions, and to watch his conduct. My experience with Tsai Yu has led to this change.

"I have never seen," said the Master, "a man of inflexible firmness." Some one thereupon mentioned Shin Ch'ang, a disciple. "Ch'ang," said he, "is wanton; where do you get at his inflexibleness?"

Tsz-kung made the remark: "That which I do not wish others to put upon me, I also wish not to put upon others." "Nay," said the Master, "you have not got so far as that."

The same disciple once remarked, "There may be access so as to hear the Master's literary discourses, but when he is treating of human nature and the way of Heaven, there may not be such success."

Tsz-lu, after once hearing him upon some subject, and feeling himself as yet incompetent to carry into practice what he had heard, used to be apprehensive only lest he should hear the subject revived.

Tsz-kung asked how it was that Kung Wan had come to be so styled Wan (the talented). The Master's answer was, "Because, though a man of an active nature, he was yet fond of study, and he was not ashamed to stoop to put questions to his inferiors."

Respecting Tsz-ch'an,[3] the Master said that he had four of the essential qualities of the 'superior man':—in his own private walk he was humble-minded; in serving his superiors he was deferential; in his looking after the material welfare of the people he was generously kind; and in his exaction of public service from the latter he was just.

[3] A great statesman of Confucius's time.

Speaking of Yen Ping, he said, "He was one who was happy in his mode of attaching men to him. However long the intercourse, he was always deferential to them."

Referring to Tsang Wan, he asked, "What is to be said of this man's discernment?—this man with his tortoise-house, with the pillar-heads and posts bedizened with scenes of hill and mere!"

Tsz-chang put a question relative to the chief Minister of Tsu, Tsz-wan. He said, "Three times he became chief Minister, and on none of these occasions did he betray any sign of exultation. Three times his ministry came to an end, and he showed no sign of chagrin. He used without fail to inform the new Minister as to the old mode of administration. What say you of him?"

"That he was a loyal man," said the Master.

"But was he a man of fellow-feeling?" said the disciple.

"Of that I am not sure," he answered; "how am I to get at that?"

The disciple went on to say:—"After the assassination of the prince of Ts'i by the officer Ts'ui, the latter's fellow-official Ch'in Wan, who had half a score teams of horses, gave up all, and turned his back upon him. On coming to another State, he observed, 'There are here characters somewhat like that of our minister Ts'ui,' and he turned his back upon them. Proceeding to a certain other State, he had occasion to make the same remark, and left. What say you of him?"

"That he was a pure-minded man," answered the Master.

"But was he a man of fellow-feeling?" urged the disciple.

"Of that I am not sure," he replied; "how am I to get at that?"

Ki Wan was one who thought three times over a thing before he acted. The Master hearing this of him, observed, "Twice would have been enough."

Of Ning Wu, the Master said that when matters went

well in the State he used to have his wits about him: but when they went wrong, he lost them. His intelligence might be equalled, but not his witlessness!

Once, when the Master lived in the State of Ch'in, he exclaimed, "Let me get home again! Let me get home! My school-children[4] are wild and impetuous! Though they are somewhat accomplished, and perfect in one sense in their attainments, yet they know not how to make nice discriminations."

Of Peh-I and Shuh Ts'i he said, "By the fact of their not remembering old grievances, they gradually did away with resentment."

Of Wei-shang Kau he said, "Who calls him straightforward? A person once begged some vinegar of him, and he begged it from a neighbor, and then presented him with it!"

"Fine speech," said he, "and studied mien, and superfluous show of deference—of such things Tso-k'iu Ming was ashamed. I too am ashamed of such things. Also of hiding resentment felt towards an opponent and treating him as a friend—of this kind of thing he was ashamed, and so too am I."

Attended once by the two disciples Yen Yuen and Tszlu, he said, "Come now, why not tell me, each of you, what in your hearts you are really after?"

"I should like," said Tsz-lu, "for myself and my friends and associates, carriages and horses, and to be clad in light furs! nor would I mind much if they should become the worse for wear."

"And I should like," said Yen Yuen, "to live without boasting of my abilities, and without display of meritorious deeds."

Tsz-lu then said, "I should like, sir, to hear what your heart is set upon."

[4] A familiar way of speaking of his disciples in their hearing.

The Master replied, "It is this:—in regard to old people, to give them quiet and comfort; in regard to friends and associates, to be faithful to them; in regard to the young, to treat them with fostering affection and kindness."

On one occasion the Master exclaimed, "Ah, 'tis hopeless! I have not yet seen the man who can see his errors, so as inwardly to accuse himself."

"In a small cluster of houses there may well be," said he, "some whose integrity and sincerity may compare with mine; but I yield to none in point of love of learning."

BOOK VI

More Characteristics—Wisdom—Philanthropy

OF Yen Yung, a disciple, the Master said, "Yung might indeed do for a prince!"

On being asked by this Yen Yung his opinion of a certain individual, the Master replied, "He is passable. Impetuous, though."

"But," argued the disciple, "if a man habituate himself to a reverent regard for duty—even while in his way of doing things he is impetuous—in the oversight of the people committed to his charge, is he not passable? If, on the other hand, he habituate himself to impetuosity of mind, and show it also in his way of doing things, is he not then over-impetuous?"

"You are right," said the Master.

When the Duke Ngai inquired which of the disciples were devoted to learning, Confucius answered him, "There was one Yen Hwúi who loved it—a man whose angry feelings towards any particular person he did not suffer to visit upon another; a man who would never fall into the same error twice. Unfortunately his allotted time was short, and he died, and now his like is not to be found; I have never heard of one so devoted to learning."

While Tsz-hwa, a disciple, was away on a mission to Ts'i, the disciple Yen Yu, on behalf of his mother, applied for some grain. "Give her three pecks," said the Master. He applied for more. "Give her eight, then." Yen gave her fifty times that amount. The Master said, "When Tsz-hwa went on that journey to Ts'i, he had well-fed steeds yoked

31

to his carriage, and was arrayed in light furs. I have learnt that the 'superior man' should help those whose needs are urgent, not help the rich to be more rich."

When Yuen Sz became prefect under him, he gave him nine hundred measures of grain, but the prefect declined to accept them.[1] "You must not," said the Master. "May they not be of use to the villages and hamlets around you?"

Speaking of Yen Yung again, the Master said, "If the offspring of a speckled ox be red in color, and horned, even though men may not wish to take it for sacrifice, would the spirits of the hills and streams reject it?"

Adverting to Hwúi again, he said, "For three months there would not be in his breast one thought recalcitrant against his feeling of good-will towards his fellow-men. The others may attain to this for a day or for a month, but there they end."

When asked by Ki K'ang whether Tsz-lu was fit to serve the government, the Master replied, "Tsz-lu is a man of decision: what should prevent him from serving the government?"

Asked the same question respecting Tsz-kung and Yen Yu he answered similarly, pronouncing Tsz-kung to be a man of perspicacity, and Yen Yu to be one versed in the polite arts.

When the head of the Ki family sent for Min Tsz-k'ien to make him governor of the town of Pi, that disciple said, "Politely decline for me. If the offer is renewed, then indeed I shall feel myself obliged to go and live on the further bank of the Wan."

Peh-niu had fallen ill, and the Master was inquiring after him. Taking hold of his hand held out from the win-

---

[1] At this time Confucius was Criminal Judge in his native State of Lu. Yuen Sz had been a disciple. The commentators add that this was the officer's proper salary, and that he did wrong to refuse it.

dow, he said, "It is taking him off! Alas, his appointed time has come! Such a man, and to have such an illness!"

Of Hwúi, again: "A right worthy man indeed was he! With his simple wooden dish of rice, and his one gourd-basin of drink, away in his poor back lane, in a condition too grievous for others to have endured, he never allowed his cheery spirits to droop. Aye, a right worthy soul was he!"

"It is not," Yen Yu once apologized, "that I do not take pleasure in your doctrines; it is that I am not strong enough." The Master rejoined, "It is when those who are not strong enough have made some moderate amount of progress that they fail and give up; but you are now drawing your own line for yourself."

Addressing Tsz-hiá, the Master said, "Let your scholarship be that of gentlemen, and not like that of common men."

When Tsz-yu became governor of Wu-shing, the Master said to him, "Do you find good men about you?" The reply was, "There is Tan-t'ai Mieh-ming, who when walking eschews by-paths, and who, unless there be some public function, never approaches my private residence."

"Mang Chi-fan," said the Master, "is no sounder of his own praises. During a stampede he was in the rear, and as they were about to enter the city gate he whipped up his horses, and said, ''Twas not my daring made me lag behind. My horses would not go.'"

Obiter dicta of the Master:—

"Whoever has not the glib utterance of the priest T'o, as well as the handsomeness of Prince Cháu of Sung, will find it hard to keep out of harm's way in the present age.

"Who can go out but by that door? Why walks no one by these guiding principles?

"Where plain naturalness is more in evidence than

polish, we have—the man from the country. Where polish is more in evidence than naturalness, we have—the town scribe. It is when naturalness and polish are equally evident that we have the ideal man.

"The life of a man is—his rectitude. Life without it—such may you have the good fortune to avoid!

"They who know it are not as those who love it, nor they who love it as those who rejoice in it—that is, have the fruition of their love for it.

"To the average man, and those above the average, it is possible to discourse on higher subjects; to those from the average downwards, it is not possible."

Fan Ch'i put a query about wisdom. The Master replied, "To labor for the promoting of righteous conduct among the people of the land; to be serious in regard to spiritual beings, and to hold aloof from them;—this may be called wisdom."

To a further query, about philanthropy, he replied, "Those who possess that virtue find difficulty with it at first, success later.

"Men of practical knowledge," he said, "find their gratification among the rivers of the lowland, men of sympathetic social feeling find theirs among the hills. The former are active and bustling, the latter calm and quiet. The former take their day of pleasure, the latter look to length of days."

Alluding to the States of Ts'i and Lu, he observed, that Ts'i, by one change, might attain to the condition of Lu; and that Lu, by one change, might attain to good government.

An exclamation of the Master (satirizing the times, when old terms relating to government were still used while bereft of their old meaning):—"A quart, and not a quart! *quart*, indeed! *quart*, indeed!"

Tsai Wo, a disciple, put a query. Said he, "Suppose a

philanthropic person were told, 'There's a fellow-creature down in the well!' Would he go down after him?"

"Why should he really do so?" answered the Master. "The good man, or a superior man might be induced to go, but not to go down. He may be misled, but not befooled."

"The superior man," said he, "with his wide study of books, and hedging himself round by the Rules of Propriety, is not surely, after all that, capable of overstepping his bounds."

Once when the Master had had an interview with Nan-tsz, which had scandalized his disciple Tsz-lu, he uttered the solemn adjuration, "If I have done aught amiss, may Heaven reject me! may Heaven reject me!"

"How far-reaching," said he, "is the moral excellence that flows from the Constant Mean![2] It has for a long time been rare among the people."

Tsz-kung said, "Suppose the case of one who confers benefits far and wide upon the people, and who can, in so doing, make his bounty universally felt—how would you speak of him? Might he be called philanthropic?"

The Master exclaimed, "What a work for philanthropy! He would require indeed to be a sage! He would put.into shade even Yau and Shun!—Well, a philanthropic person, desiring for himself a firm footing, is led on to give one to others; desiring for himself an enlightened perception of things, he is led on to help others to be similarly enlightened. If one could take an illustration coming closer home to us than yours, that might be made the starting-point for speaking about philanthropy."

[2] The doctrine afterwards known by that name, and which gave its title to a Confucian treatise.

BOOK VII

Characteristics of Confucius—An Incident

SAID the Master:—

"I, as a transmitter[1] and not an originator, and as one who believes in and loves the ancients, venture to compare myself with our old P'ang.

"What find you indeed in me?—a quiet brooder and memorizer; a student never satiated with learning; an unwearied monitor of others!

"The things which weigh heavily upon my mind are these—failure to improve in the virtues, failure in discussion of what is learnt, inability to walk according to knowledge received as to what is right and just, inability also to reform what has been amiss."

In his hours of recreation and refreshment the Master's manner was easy and unconstrained, affable and winning.

Once he exclaimed, "Alas! I must be getting very feeble; 'tis long since I have had a repetition of the dreams in which I used to see the Duke of Chow.[2]

"Concentrate the mind," said he, "upon the Good Way.

"Maintain firm hold upon Virtue.

"Rely upon Philanthropy.

"Find recreation in the Arts.[3]

---

[1] In reference to his editing the six Classics of his time.

[2] This was one of his "beloved ancients," famous for what he did in helping to found the dynasty of Chow, a man of great political wisdom, a scholar also, and poet. It was the "dream" of Confucius's life to restore the country to the condition in which the Duke of Chow left it.

[3] These were six in number, viz.: Ceremonial, Music, Archery, Horsemanship, Language, and Calculation.

"I have never withheld instruction from any, even from those who have come for it with the smallest offering.

"No subject do I broach, however, to those who have no eager desire to learn; no encouraging hint do I give to those who show no anxiety to speak out their ideas; nor have I anything more to say to those who, after I have made clear one corner of the subject, cannot from that give me the other three."

If the Master was taking a meal, and there were any in mourning beside him, he would not eat to the full.

On one day on which he had wept, on that day he would not sing.

Addressing his favorite disciple, he said, "To you only and myself it has been given to do this—to go when called to serve, and to go back into quiet retirement when released from office."

Tsz-lu, hearing the remark said, "But if, sir, you had the handling of the army of one of the greater States,[4] whom would you have associated with you in that case?"

The Master answered:—

"Not the one 'who'll rouse the tiger,'
Not the one 'who'll wade the Ho;'

not the man who can die with no regret. He must be one who should watch over affairs with apprehensive caution, a man fond of strategy, and of perfect skill and effectiveness in it."

As to wealth, he remarked, "If wealth were an object that I could go in quest of, I should do so even if I had to take a whip and do grooms' work. But seeing that it is not, I go after those objects for which I have a liking."

Among matters over which he exercised great caution were times of fasting, war, and sickness.

When he was in the State of Ts'i, and had heard the

[4] Lit., three forces. Each force consisted of 12,500 men, and three of such forces were the equipment of a greater State.

ancient Shau music, he lost all perception of the taste of his meat. "I had no idea," said he, "that music could have been brought to this pitch."

In the course of conversation Yen Yu said, "Does the Master take the part of the Prince of Wei?" "Ah yes!" said Tsz-kung, "I will go and ask him that."

On going in to him, that disciple began, "What sort of men were Peh-I and Shuh Ts'i?" "Worthies of the olden time," the Master replied. "Had they any feelings of resentment?" was the next question. "Their aim and object," he answered, "was that of doing the duty which every man owes to his fellows, and they succeeded in doing it;—what room further for feelings of resentment?" The questioner on coming out said, "The Master does not take his part."

"With a meal of coarse rice," said the Master, "and with water to drink, and my bent arm for my pillow—even thus I can find happiness. Riches and honors without righteousness are to me as fleeting clouds."

"Give me several years more to live," said he, "and after fifty years' study of the 'Book of Changes' I might come to be free from serious error."

The Master's regular subjects of discourse were the "Books of the Odes" and "History," and the up-keeping of the Rules of Propriety. On all of these he regularly discoursed.

The Duke of Shih questioned Tsz-lu about Confucius, and the latter did not answer.

Hearing of this, the Master said, "Why did you not say, He is a man with a mind so intent on his pursuits that he forgets his food, and finds such pleasure in them that he forgets his troubles, and does not know that old age is coming upon him?"

"As I came not into life with any knowledge of it," he said, "and as my likings are for what is old, I busy myself in seeking knowledge there."

Strange occurrences, exploits of strength, deeds of lawlessness, references to spiritual beings—such-like matters the Master avoided in conversation.

"Let there," he said, "be three men walking together: from that number I should be sure to find my instructors; for what is good in them I should choose out and follow, and what is not good I should modify."

On one occasion he exclaimed, "Heaven begat Virtue in me; what can man do unto me?"

To his disciples he once said, "Do you look upon me, my sons, as keeping anything secret from you? I hide nothing from you. I do nothing that is not manifest to your eyes, my disciples. That is so with me."

Four things there were which he kept in view in his teaching—scholarliness, conduct of life, honesty, faithfulness.

"It is not given to me," he said, "to meet with a sage; let me but behold a man of superior mind, and that will suffice. Neither is it given to me to meet with a good man; let me but see a man of constancy, and it will suffice. It is difficult for persons to have constancy, when they pretend to have that which they are destitute of, to be full when they are empty, to do things on a grand scale when their means are contracted!"

When the Master fished with hook and line, he did not also use a net. When out with his bow, he would never shoot at game in cover.

"Some there may be," said he, "who do things in ignorance of what they do. I am not of these. There is an alternative way of knowing things, viz.—to sift out the good from the many things one hears, and follow it; and to keep in memory the many things one sees."

Pupils from Hu-hiang were difficult to speak with. One youth came to interview the Master, and the disciples were in doubt whether he ought to have been seen. "Why so much ado," said the Master, "at my merely permitting his approach, and not rather at my allowing him to draw back? If a man have cleansed himself in order to come and see me, I receive him as such; but I do not undertake for what he will do when he goes away."

"Is the philanthropic spirit far to seek, indeed?" the Master exclaimed; "I wish for it, and it is with me!"

The Minister of Crime in the State of Ch'in asked Confucius whether Duke Ch'au, of Lu was acquainted with the Proprieties; and he answered, "Yes, he knows them."

When Confucius had withdrawn, the minister bowed to Wu-ma K'i, a disciple, and motioned to him to come forward. He said, "I have heard that superior men show no partiality; are they, too, then, partial? That prince took for his wife a lady of the Wu family, having the same surname as himself, and had her named 'Lady Tsz of Wu, the elder.' If he knows the Proprieties, then who does not?"

The disciple reported this to the Master, who thereupon remarked, "Well for me! If I err in any way, others are sure to know of it."

When the Master was in company with any one who sang, and who sang well, he must needs have the song over again, and after that would join in it.

"Although in letters," he said, "I may have none to compare with me, yet in my personification of the 'superior man' I have not as yet been successful."

" 'A Sage and a Philanthropist?' How should I have the ambition?" said he. "All that I can well be called is this— An insatiable student, an unwearied teacher;—this, and no more."—"Exactly what we, your disciples, cannot by any learning manage to be," said Kung-si Hwa.

Once when the Master was seriously ill, Tsz-lu requested to be allowed to say prayers for him. "Are such available?" asked the Master. "Yes," said he; "and the Manual of Prayers says, 'Pray to the spirits above and to those here below.'"

"My praying has been going on a long while," said the Master.

"Lavish living," he said, "renders men disorderly; miserliness makes them hard. Better, however, the hard than the disorderly."

Again, "The man of superior mind is placidly composed; the small-minded man is in a constant state of perturbation."

The Master was gentle, yet could be severe; had an overawing presence, yet was not violent; was deferential, yet easy.

BOOK VIII

Sayings of Tsang—Sentences of the Master

SPEAKING of T'ai-pih the Master said that he might be pronounced a man of the highest moral excellence; for he allowed the empire to pass by him onwards to a third heir; while the people, in their ignorance of his motives, were unable to admire him for so doing.

"Without the Proprieties," said the Master, "we have these results: for deferential demeanor, a worried one; for calm attentiveness, awkward bashfulness; for manly conduct, disorderliness; for straightforwardness, perversity.

"When men of rank show genuine care for those nearest to them in blood, the people rise to the duty of neighborliness and sociability. And when old friendships among them are not allowed to fall off, there will be a cessation of underhand practices among the people."

The Scholar Tsang was once unwell, and calling his pupils to him he said to them, "Disclose to view my feet and my hands. What says the Ode?—

> 'Act as from a sense of danger,
>   With precaution and with care,
> As a yawning gulf o'erlooking,
>   As on ice that scarce will bear.'

At all times, my children, I know how to keep myself free from bodily harm."

Again, during an illness of his, Mang King, an official, went to ask after him. The Scholar had some conversation with him, in the course of which he said—

" 'Doleful the cries of a dying bird,
Good the last words of a dying man.'

There are three points which a man of rank in the management of his duties should set store upon:—A lively manner and deportment, banishing both severity and laxity; a frank and open expression of countenance, allied closely with sincerity; and a tone in his utterances utterly free from any approach to vulgarity and impropriety. As to matters of bowls and dishes, leave such things to those who are charged with the care of them."

Another saying of the Scholar Tsang: "I once had a friend who, though he possessed ability, would go questioning men of none, and though surrounded by numbers, would go with his questions to isolated individuals; who also, whatever he might have, appeared as if he were without it, and, with all his substantial acquirements, made as though his mind were a mere blank; and when insulted would not retaliate;—this was ever his way."

Again he said: "The man that is capable of being intrusted with the charge of a minor on the throne, and given authority over a large territory, and who, during the important term of his superintendence cannot be forced out of his position, is not such a 'superior man'? That he is, indeed."

Again:—"The learned official must not be without breadth and power of endurance: the burden is heavy, and the way is long.

"Suppose that he take his duty to his fellow-men as his peculiar burden, is that not indeed a heavy one? And since only with death it is done with, is not the way long?"

Sentences of the Master:—

"From the 'Book of Odes' we receive impulses; from the 'Book of the Rules,' stability; from the 'Book on Music,' refinement.[1]

[1] Comparison of three of the Classics: the "Shi-King," the "Li Ki," and the "Yoh." The last is lost.

"The people may be put into the way they should go, though they may not be put into the way of understanding it.

"The man who likes bravery, and yet groans under poverty, has mischief in him. So, too, has the misanthrope, groaning at any severity shown towards him.

"Even if a person were adorned with the gifts of the Duke of Chow, yet if he were proud and avaricious, all the rest of his qualities would not indeed be worth looking at.

"Not easily found is the man who, after three years' study, has failed to come upon some fruit of his toil.

"The really faithful lover of learning holds fast to the Good Way till death.

"He will not go into a State in which a downfall is imminent, nor take up his abode in one where disorder reigns. When the empire is well ordered he will show himself; when not, he will hide himself away. Under a good government it will be a disgrace to him if he remain in poverty and low estate; under a bad one, it would be equally disgraceful to him to hold riches and honors.

"If not occupying the office, devise not the policy.

"When the professor Chi began his duties, how grand the finale of the First of the Odes used to be! How it rang in one's ears!

"I cannot understand persons who are enthusiastic and yet not straightforward; nor those who are ignorant and yet not attentive; nor again those folks who are simpleminded and yet untrue.

"Learn, as if never overtaking your object, and yet as if apprehensive of losing it.

"How sublime was the handling of the empire by Shun and Yu!—it was as nothing to them!

"How great was Yau as a prince! Was he not sublime! Say that Heaven only is great, then was Yau alone after its pattern! How profound was he! The people could not find a name for him. How sublime in his achievements! How brilliant in his scholarly productions!"

Shun had for his ministers five men, by whom he ordered the empire.

King Wu (in his day) stated that he had ten men as assistants for the promotion of order.

With reference to these facts Confucius observed, "Ability is hard to find. Is it not so indeed? During the three years' interregnum between Yau and Shun there was more of it than in the interval before this present dynasty appeared. There were, at this latter period, one woman, and nine men only.

"When two-thirds of the empire were held by King Wan, he served with that portion the House of Yin. We speak of the virtue of the House of Chow; we may say, indeed, that it reached the pinnacle of excellence."

"As to Yu," added the Master, "I can find no flaw in him. Living on meagre food and drink; yet providing to the utmost in his filial offerings to the spirits of the dead! Dressing in coarse garments; yet most elegant when vested in his sacrificial apron and coronet! Dwelling in a poor palace; yet exhausting his energies over those boundary-ditches and watercourses! I can find no flaw in Yu."

BOOK IX

His Favorite Disciple's Opinion of Him

TOPICS on which the Master rarely spoke were—Advantage, and Destiny, and Duty of man to man.

A man of the village of Tah-hiang exclaimed of him, "A great man is Confucius!—a man of extensive learning, and yet in nothing has he quite made himself a name!"

The Master heard of this, and mentioning it to his disciples he said. "What then shall I take in hand? Shall I become a carriage driver, or an archer? Let me be a driver!"

"The sacrificial cap," he once said, "should, according to the Rules, be of linen; but in these days it is of pure silk. However, as it is economical, I do as all do.

"The Rule says, 'Make your bow when at the lower end of the hall'; but nowadays the bowing is done at the upper part. This is great freedom; and I, though I go in opposition to the crowd, bow when at the lower end."

The Master barred four words:—he would have no "shall's," no "must's," no "certainly's," no "I's."

Once, in the town of K'wang fearing that his life was going to be taken, the Master exclaimed, "King Wan is dead and gone; but is not '*wan*'[1] with you here? If Heaven be about to allow this '*wan*' to perish, then they who sur-

---

[1] "Wan" was the honorary appellation of the great sage and ruler, whose praise is in the "Shi-King" as one of the founders of the Chow dynasty, and the term represented civic talent and virtues, as distinct from Wu, the martial talent—the latter being the honorary title of his son and successor. "Wan" also often stands for literature, and polite accomplishments. Here Confucius simply means, "If you kill me, you kill a sage."

46

vive its decease will get no benefit from it. But so long as Heaven does not allow it to perish, what can the men of K'wang do to me?"

A high State official, after questioning Tsz-kung, said, "Your Master is a sage, then? How many and what varied abilities must be his!"

The disciple replied, "Certainly Heaven is allowing him full opportunities of becoming a sage, in addition to the fact that his abilities are many and varied."

When the Master heard of this he remarked, "Does that high official know me? In my early years my position in life was low, and hence my ability in many ways, though exercised in trifling matters. In the gentleman is there indeed such variety of ability? No."

From this, the disciple Lau used to say, " 'Twas a saying of the Master: 'At a time when I was not called upon to use them, I acquired my proficiency in the polite arts.' "

"Am I, indeed," said the Master, "possessed of knowledge? I know nothing. Let a vulgar fellow come to me with a question—a man with an emptyish head—I may thrash out with him the matter from end to end, and exhaust myself in doing it!"

"Ah!" exclaimed he once, "the phœnix does not come! and no symbols issue from the river! May I not as well give up?"

Whenever the Master met with a person in mourning, or with one in full-dress cap and kirtle, or with a blind person, although they might be young persons, he would make a point of rising on their appearance, or, if crossing their path, would do so with quickened step!

Once Yen Yuen exclaimed with a sigh (with reference to the Master's doctrines), "If I look up to them, they are ever the higher; if I try to penetrate them, they are ever the harder; if I gaze at them as if before my eyes, lo, they are behind me!— Gradually and gently the Master with skill lures men on. By literary lore he gave me breadth; by the Rules of Propriety he narrowed me down. When I desire a respite, I find it impossible; and after I have exhausted my powers, there seems to be something standing straight up in front of me, and though I have the mind to make towards it I make no advance at all."

Once when the Master was seriously ill, Tsz-lu induced the other disciples to feign they were high officials acting in his service. During a respite from his malady the Master exclaimed, "Ah! how long has Tsz-lu's conduct been false? Whom should I delude, if I were to pretend to have officials under me, having none? Should I deceive Heaven? Besides, were I to die, I would rather die in the hands of yourselves, my disciples, than in the hands of officials. And though I should fail to have a grand funeral over me, I should hardly be left on my death on the public highway, should I?"

Tsz-kung one said to him, "Here is a fine gem. Would you guard it carefully in a casket and store it away, or seek a good price for it and sell it?" "Sell it, indeed," said the Master—"that would I; but I should wait for the bidder."

The Master protested he would "go and live among the nine wild tribes."

"A rude life," said some one;—"how could you put up with it?"

"What rudeness would there be," he replied, "if a 'superior man' was living in their midst?"

Once he remarked, "After I came back from Wei to Lu the music was put right, and each of the Festal Odes and Hymns was given its appropriate place and use."

"Ah! which one of these following," he asked on one occasion, "are to be found exemplified in me—proper service rendered to superiors when abroad; duty to father and elder brother when at home; duty that shrinks from no exertion when dear ones die; and keeping free from the confusing effects of wine?"

Standing once on the bank of a mountain stream, he said (musingly), "Like this are those that pass away—no cessation, day or night!"

Other sayings:—

"Take an illustraticn from the making of a hill. A simple basketful is wanting to complete it, and the work stops. So I stop short.

"Take an illustration from the levelling of the ground. Suppose again just one basketful is left, when the work has so progressed. There I desist!

"Ah! it was Hwúi, was it not? who, when I had given him his lesson, was the unflagging one!

"Alas for Hwúi! I saw him ever making progress. I never saw him stopping short.

"Blade, but no bloom—or else bloom, but no produce; aye, that is the way with some!

"Reverent regard is due to youth. How know we what difference there may be in them in the future from what they are now? Yet when they have reached the age of forty or fifty, and are still unknown in the world, then indeed they are no more worthy of such regard.

"Can any do otherwise than assent to words said to them by way of correction? Only let them reform by such advice, and it will then be reckoned valuable. Can any be other than pleased with words of gentle suasion? Only let them comply with them fully, and such also will be accounted valuable. With those who are pleased without so complying, and those who assent but do not reform, I can do nothing at all.

"Give prominent place to loyalty and sincerity.

"Have no associates in study who are not advanced somewhat like yourself.

"When you have erred, be not afraid to correct yourself.

"It may be possible to seize and carry off the chief commander of a large army, but not possible so to rob one poor fellow of his will.

"One who stands—clad in hempen robe, the worse for wear—among others clad in furs of fox and badger, and yet unabashed—'tis Tsz-lu, that, is it not?"

Tsz-lu used always to be humming over the lines—

> "From envy and enmity free,
>   What deed doth he other than good?"

"How should such a rule of life," asked the Master, "be sufficient to make any one good?"

"When the year grows chilly, we know the pine and cypress are the last to fade.

"The wise escape doubt; the good-hearted, trouble; the bold, apprehension.

"Some may study side by side, and yet be asunder when they come to the logic of things. Some may go on together in this latter course, but be wide apart in the standards they reach in it. Some, again, may together reach the same standard, and yet be diverse in weight of character."

> "The blossom is out on the cherry tree,
>   With a flutter on every spray.
> Dost think that my thoughts go not out to thee?
>   Ah, why art thou far away!"

Commenting on these lines the Master said, "There can hardly have been much 'thought going out.' What does distance signify?"

BOOK X

Confucius in Private and Official Life

In his own village, Confucius presented a somewhat plain and simple appearance, and looked unlike a man who possessed ability of speech.

But in the ancestral temple, and at Court, he spoke with the fluency and accuracy of a debater, but ever guardedly.

At Court, conversing with the lower order of great officials, he spoke somewhat firmly and directly; with those of the higher order his tone was somewhat more affable.

When the prince was present he was constrainedly reverent in his movements, and showed a proper degree of grave dignity in demeanor.

Whenever the prince summoned him to act as usher to the Court, his look would change somewhat, and he would make as though he were turning round to do obeisance.

He would salute those among whom he took up his position, using the right hand or the left, and holding the skirts of his robe in proper position before and behind. He would make his approaches with quick step, and with elbows evenly bent outwards.

When the visitor withdrew, he would not fail to report the execution of his commands, with the words, "The visitor no longer looks back."

When he entered the palace gate, it was with the body somewhat bent forward, almost as though he could not be admitted. When he stood still, this would never happen in the middle of the gateway; nor when moving about would he ever tread on the threshold. When passing the throne, his look would change somewhat, he would turn aside and make a sort of obeisance, and the words he spoke seemed as though he were deficient in utterance.

On going up the steps to the audience chamber, he would gather up with both hands the ends of his robe, and walk with his body bent somewhat forward, holding back his breath like one in whom respiration has ceased. On coming out, after descending one step his countenance would relax and assume an appearance of satisfaction. Arrived at the bottom, he would go forward with quick step, his elbows evenly bent outwards, back to his position, constrainedly reverent in every movement.

When holding the sceptre in his hand, his body would be somewhat bent forward, as if he were not equal to carrying it; wielding it now higher, as in a salutation, now lower, as in the presentation of a gift; his look would also be changed and appear awestruck; and his gait would seem retarded, as if he were obeying some restraining hand behind.

When he presented the gifts of ceremony, he would assume a placid expression of countenance. At the private interview he would be cordial and affable.

The good man would use no purple or violet colors for the facings of his dress.[1] Nor would he have red or orange color for his undress.[2] For the hot season he wore a singlet, of either coarse or fine texture, but would also feel bound to have an outer garment covering it. For his black robe he had lamb's wool; for his white one, fawn's fur; and for his yellow one, fox fur. His furred undress robe was longer, but the right sleeve was shortened. He would needs have his sleeping-dress one and a half times his own

---

[1] Because, it is said, such colors were adopted in fasting and mourning.
[2] Because they did not belong to the five correct colors (viz. green, yellow, carnation, white, and black), and were affected more by females.

length. For ordinary home wear he used thick substantial fox or badger furs. When he left off mourning, he would wear all his girdle trinkets. His kirtle in front, when it was not needed for full cover, he must needs have cut down. He would never wear his (black) lamb's-wool, or a dark-colored cap, when he went on visits of condolence to mourners.[3] On the first day of the new moon, he must have on his Court dress and to Court. When observing his fasts, he made a point of having bright, shiny garments, made of linen. He must also at such times vary his food, and move his seat to another part of his dwelling-room.

As to his food, he never tired of rice so long as it was clean and pure, nor of hashed meats when finely minced. Rice spoiled by damp, and sour, he would not touch, nor tainted fish, nor bad meat, nor aught of a bad color or smell, nor aught overdone in cooking, nor aught out of season. Neither would he eat anything that was not properly cut, or that lacked its proper seasonings. Although there might be an abundance of meat before him, he would not allow a preponderance of it to rob the rice of its beneficial effect in nutrition. Only in the matter of wine did he set himself no limit, yet he never drank so much as to confuse himself. Tradesmen's wines, and dried meats from the market, he would not touch. Ginger he would never have removed from the table during a meal. He was not a great eater. Meat from the sacrifices at the prince's temple he would never put aside till the following day. The meat of his own offerings he would never give out after three days' keeping, for after that time none were to eat it.

At his meals he would not enter into discussions; and when reposing (afterwards) he would not utter a word.

[3] Since white was, as it is still, the mourning color.

Even should his meal consist only of coarse rice and vegetable broth or melons, he would make an offering, and never fail to do so religiously.

He would never sit on a mat that was not straight.

After a feast among his villagers, he would wait before going away until the old men had left.

When the village people were exorcising the pests, he would put on his Court robes and stand on the steps of his hall to receive them.

When he was sending a message of inquiry to a person in another State, he would bow twice on seeing the messenger off.

Ki K'ang once sent him a present of some medicine. He bowed, and received it; but remarked, "Until I am quite sure of its properties I must not venture to taste it."

Once when the stabling was destroyed by fire, he withdrew from the Court, and asked, "Is any person injured?" —without inquiring as to the horses.

Whenever the prince sent him a present of food, he was particular to set his mat in proper order, and would be the first one to taste it. If the prince's present was one of raw meat, he must needs have it cooked, and make an oblation of it. If the gift were a live animal, he would be sure to keep it and care for it.

When he was in waiting, and at a meal with the prince, the prince would make the offering,[4] and he (the Master) was the pregustator.

When unwell, and the prince came to see him, he would arrange his position so that his head inclined towards the east, would put over him his Court robes, and draw his girdle across them.

When summoned by order of the prince, he would start off without waiting for his horses to be put to.

‘The act of "grace," before eating.

On his entry into the Grand Temple, he inquired about everything connected with its usages.

If a friend died, and there were no near relatives to take him to, he would say, "Let him be buried from my house."

For a friend's gift—unless it consisted of meat that had been offered in sacrifice—he would not bow, even if it were a carriage and horses.

In repose he did not lie like one dead. In his home life he was not formal in his manner.

Whenever he met with a person in mourning, even though it were a familiar acquaintance, he would be certain to change his manner; and when he met with any one in full-dress cap, or with any blind person, he would also unfailingly put on a different look, even though he were himself in undress at the time.

In saluting any person wearing mourning he would bow forwards towards the front bar of his carriage; in the same manner he would also salute the bearer of a census-register.

When a sumptuous banquet was spread before him, a different expression would be sure to appear in his features, and he would rise up from his seat.

At a sudden thunder-clap, or when the wind grew furious, his look would also invariably be changed.

On getting into his car, he would never fail (first) to stand up erect, holding on by the strap. When in the car, he would never look about, nor speak hastily, nor bring one hand to the other.

> "Let one but make a movement in his face,
>   And the bird will rise and seek some safer place."

Apropos of this, he said, "Here is a hen-pheasant from Shan Liang—and in season! and in season!" After Tsz-lu had got it prepared, he smelt it thrice, and then rose up from his seat.

BOOK XI

Comparative Worth of His Disciples

"THE first to make progress in the Proprieties and in Music," said the Master, "are plain countrymen; after them, the men of higher standing. If I had to employ any of them, I should stand by the former."

"Of those," said he, "who were about me when I was in the Ch'in and Ts'ai States, not one now is left to approach my door."

"As for Hwúi,"[1] said the Master, "he is not one to help me on: there is nothing I say but he is not well satisfied with."

"What a dutiful son was Min Tsz-k'ien!" he exclaimed. "No one finds occasion to differ from what his parents and brothers have said of him."

Nan Yung used to repeat three times over the lines in the Odes about the white sceptre. Confucius caused his own elder brother's daughter to be given in marriage to him.

When Ki K'ang inquired which of the disciples were fond of learning, Confucius answered him, "There was one Yen Hwúi who was fond of it; but unfortunately his allotted time was short, and he died; and now his like is not to be found."

When Yen Yuen died, his father, Yen Lu, begged for the Master's carriage in order to get a shell for his coffin.

[1] The men of virtuous life were Yen Yuen (Hwúi), Min Tsz-k'ien, Yen Pih-niu, and Chung-kung (Yen Yung); the speakers and debaters were Tsai Wo and Tsz-kung; the (capable) government servants were Yen Yu and Tsz-lu; the literary students, Tsz-yu and Tsz-hiá.

"Ability or no ability," said the Master, "every father still speaks of 'my son.' When my own son Li died, and the coffin for him had no shell to it, I know I did not go on foot to get him one; but that was because I was, though retired, in the wake of the ministers, and could not therefore well do so."

On the death of Yen Yuen the Master exclaimed, "Ah me! Heaven is ruining me, Heaven is ruining me!"

On the same occasion, his wailing for that disciple becoming excessive, those who were about him said, "Sir, this is too much!"—"Too much?" said he; "if I am not to do so for him, then—for whom else?"

The disciples then wished for the deceased a grand funeral. The Master could not on his part consent to this. They nevertheless gave him one. Upon this he remarked, "He used to look upon me as if I were his father. I could never, however, look on him as a son. 'Twas not my mistake, but yours, my children."

Tsz-lu propounded a question about ministering to the spirits of the departed. The Master replied, "Where there is scarcely the ability to minister to living men, how shall there be ability to minister to the spirits?" On his venturing to put a question concerning death, he answered, "Where there is scarcely any knowledge about life, how shall there be any about death?"

The disciple Min was by his side, looking affable and bland; Tsz-lu also, looking careless and intrepid; and Yen Yu and Tsz-kung, firm and precise. The Master was cheery. "One like Tsz-lu there," said he, "does not come to a natural end."

Some persons in Lu were taking measures in regard to the Long Treasury House. Min Tsz-k'ien observed, "How if it were repaired on the old lines?" The Master upon this remarked, "This fellow is not a talker, but when he does speak he is bound to hit the mark!"

"There is Yu's harpsichord," exclaimed the Master—
"what is it doing at my door?" On seeing, however, some
disrespect shown to him by the other disciples, he added,
"Yu has got as far as the top of the hall; only he has not
yet entered the house."

Tsz-kung asked which was the worthier of the two—
Tsz-chang or Tsz-hiá. "The former," answered the Master,
"goes beyond the mark; the latter falls short of it."

"So then Tsz-chang is the better of the two, is he?" said
he.

"To go too far," he replied, "is about the same as to fall
short."

The Chief of the Ki family was a wealthier man than
the Duke of Chow had been, and yet Yen Yu gathered
and hoarded for him, increasing his wealth more and more.

"He is no follower of mine," said the Master. "It would
serve him right, my children, to sound the drum, and set
upon him."

Characteristics of four disciples:—Tsz-káu was simpleminded; Tsang Si, a dullard; Tsz-chang, full of airs; Tsz-lu,
rough.

"As to Hwúi," said the Master, "he comes near to perfection, while frequently in great want. Tsz-kung does not
submit to the appointments of Heaven; and yet his goods
are increased;—he is often successful in his calculations."

Tsz-chang wanted to know some marks of the naturally
Good Man.

"He does not walk in others' footprints," said the Master; "yet he does not get beyond the hall into the house."

Once the Master said, "Because we allow that a man's
words have something genuine in them, are they necessarily those of a superior man? or words carrying only an
outward semblance and show of gravity?"

Tsz-lu put a question about the practice of precepts one
has heard. The Master's reply was, "In a case where there

is a father or elder brother still left with you, how should you practise all you hear?"

When, however, the same question was put to him by Yen Yu, his reply was, "Yes; do so."

Kung-si Hwa animadverted upon this to the Master. "Tsz-lu asked you, sir," said he, "about the practice of what one has learnt, and you said, 'There may be a father or elder brother still alive'; but when Yen Yu asked the same question, you answered, 'Yes, do so.' I am at a loss to understand you, and venture to ask what you meant."

The Master replied, "Yen Yu backs out of his duties; therefore I push him on. Tsz-lu has forwardness enough for them both; therefore I hold him back."

On the occasion of that time of fear in K'wang, Yen Yuen having fallen behind, the Master said to him (afterwards), "I took it for granted you were a dead man." "How should I dare to die," said he, "while you, sir, still lived?"

On Ki Tsz-jen putting to him a question anent Tsz-lu and Yen Yu, as to whether they might be called "great ministers," the Master answered, "I had expected your question, sir, to be about something extraordinary, and lo! it is only about these two. Those whom we call 'great ministers' are such as serve their prince conscientiously, and who, when they cannot do so, retire. At present, as regards the two you ask about, they may be called 'qualified ministers.'"

"Well, are they then," he asked, "such as will follow their leader?"

"They would not follow him who should slay his father and his prince!" was the reply.

Through the intervention of Tsz-lu, Tsz-káu was being appointed governor of Pi.

"You are spoiling a good man's son," said the Master.

Tsz-lu rejoined, "But he will have the people and their

superiors to gain experience from, and there will be the altars; what need to read books? He can become a student afterwards."

"Here is the reason for my hatred of glib-tongued people," said the Master.

On one occasion Tsz-lu, Tsang Sin, Yen Yu, and Kung-si Hwa were sitting near him. He said to them, "Though I may be a day older than you, do not (for the moment) regard me as such. While you are living this unoccupied life you are saying, 'We do not become known.' Now suppose some one got to know you, what then?"

Tsz-lu—first to speak—at once answered, "Give me a State of large size and armament, hemmed in and hampered by other larger States, the population augmented by armies and regiments, causing a dearth in it of food of all kinds; give me charge of that State, and in three years' time I should make a brave country of it, and let it know its place."

The Master smiled at him. "Yen," said he, "how would it be with you?"

"Give me," said Yen, "a territory of sixty or seventy li square, or of fifty or sixty square; put me in charge of that, and in three years I should make the people sufficiently prosperous. As regards their knowledge of ceremonial or music, I should wait for superior men to teach them that."

"And with you, Kung-si, how would it be?"

This disciple's reply was, "I have nothing to say about my capabilities for such matters; my wish is to learn. I should like to be a junior assistant, in dark rob and cap, at the services of the ancestral temple, and at the Grand Receptions of the Princes by the Sovereign."

"And with you, Tsang Sin?"

This disciple was strumming on his harpsichord, but now the twanging ceased, he turned from the instrument, rose to his feet, and answered thus: "Something different from the choice of these three." "What harm?" said the Master; "I want each one of you to tell me what his heart is set upon." "Well, then," said he, "give me—in the latter part of spring—dressed in full spring-tide attire—in company with five or six young fellows of twenty,[2] or six or seven lads under that age, to do the ablutions in the I stream, enjoy a breeze in the rain-dance,[3] and finish up with songs on the road home."

The Master drew in his breath, sighed, and exclaimed, "Ah, I take with you!"

The three other disciples having gone out, leaving Tsang Sin behind, the latter said, "What think you of the answers of those three?"—"Well, each told me what was uppermost in his mind," said the Master;—"simply that."

"Why did you smile at Tsz-lu, sir?"

"I smiled at him because to have the charge of a State requires due regard to the Rules of Propriety, and his words betrayed a lack of modesty."

"But Yen, then—he had a State in view, had he not?"

"I should like to be shown a territory such as he described which does not amount to a State."

"But had not Kung-si also a State in view?"

"What are ancestral temples and Grand Receptions, but for the feudal lords to take part in? If Kung-si were to become an unimportant assistant at these functions, who could become an important one?"

[2] Lit., capped ones. At twenty they underwent the ceremony of capping, and were considered men.

[3] I.e., before the altars, where offerings were placed with prayer for rain. A religious dance.

BOOK XII

The Master's Answers—Philanthropy—Friendships

YEN YUEN was asking about man's proper regard for his fellow-man. The Master said to him, "Self-control, and a habit of falling back upon propriety, virtually effect it. Let these conditions be fulfilled for one day, and every one round will betake himself to the duty. Is it to begin in one's self, or think you, indeed! it is to begin in others?"

"I wanted you to be good enough," said Yen Yuen, "to give me a brief synopsis of it."

Then said the Master, "Without Propriety use not your eyes; without it use not your ears, nor your tongue, nor a limb of your body."

"I may be lacking in diligence," said Yen Yuen, "but with your favor I will endeavor to carry out this advice."

Chung-kung asked about man's proper regard for his fellows.

To him the Master replied thus: "When you go forth from your door, be as if you were meeting some guest of importance. When you are making use of the common people (for State purposes), be as if you were taking part in a great religious function. Do not set before others what you do not desire yourself. Let there be no resentful feelings against you when you are away in the country, and none when at home."

"I may lack diligence," said Chung-kung, "but with your favor I will endeavor to carry out this advice."

Sz-ma Niu asked the like question. The answer he received was this: "The words of the man who has a proper regard for his fellows are uttered with difficulty."

"'His words—uttered with difficulty?'" he echoed, in surprise. "Is that what is meant by proper regard for one's fellow-creatures?"

"Where there is difficulty in doing," the Master replied, "will there not be some difficulty in utterance?"

The same disciple put a question about the "superior man." "Superior men," he replied, "are free from trouble and apprehension."

"'Free from trouble and apprehension!'" said he. "Does that make them 'superior men'?"

The Master added, "Where there is found, upon introspection, to be no chronic disease, how shall there be any trouble? how shall there be any apprehension?"

The same disciple, being in trouble, remarked, "I am alone in having no brother, while all else have theirs—younger or elder."

Tsz-hiá said to him, "I have heard this: 'Death and life have destined times; wealth and honors rest with Heaven. Let the superior man keep watch over himself without ceasing, showing deference to others, with propriety of manners—and all within the four seas will be his brethren. How should he be distressed for lack of brothers!'" [1]

Tsz-chang asked what sort of man might be termed "enlightened."

The Master replied, "That man with whom drenching slander and cutting calumny gain no currency may well be called enlightened. Ay, he with whom such things make no way may well be called enlightened in the extreme."

Tsz-kung put a question relative to government. In reply the Master mentioned three essentials:—sufficient food, sufficient armament, and the people's confidence.

[1] From Confucius, it is generally thought.

"But," said the disciple, "if you cannot really have all three, and one has to be given up, which would you give up first?"

"The armament," he replied.

"And if you are obliged to give up one of the remaining two, which would it be?"

"The food," said he. "Death has been the portion of all men from of old. Without the people's trust nothing can stand."

Kih Tsz-shing once said, "Give me the inborn qualities of a gentleman, and I want no more. How are such to come from book-learning?"

Tsz-kung exclaimed, "Ah! sir, I regret to hear such words from you. A gentleman!—But 'a team of four can ne'er o'ertake the tongue!' Literary accomplishments are much the same as inborn qualities, and inborn qualities as literary accomplishments. A tiger's or leopard's skin without the hair might be a dog's or sheep's when so made bare."

Duke Ngai was consulting Yu Joh. Said he, "It is a year of dearth, and there is an insufficiency for Ways and Means—what am I to do?"

"Why not apply the Tithing Statute?" said the minister.

"But two tithings would not be enough for my purposes," said the duke; "what would be the good of applying the Statute?"

The minister replied, "So long as the people have enough left for themselves, who of them will allow their prince to be without enough? But—when the people have not enough, who will allow their prince all that he wants?"

Tsz-chang was asking how the standard of virtue was to be raised, and how to discern what was illusory or misleading. The Master's answer was, "Give a foremost place to honesty and faithfulness, and tread the path of righteousness, and you will raise the standard of virtue. As to discerning what is illusory, here is an example of an illusion:—Whom you love you wish to live; whom you hate you wish to die. To have wished the same person to live and also to be dead—there is an illusion for you."

Duke King of Ts'i consulted Confucius about government. His answer was, "Let a prince be a prince, and ministers be ministers; let fathers be fathers, and sons be sons."

"Good!" exclaimed the duke; "truly if a prince fail to be a prince, and ministers to be ministers, and if fathers be not fathers, and sons not sons, then, even though I may have my allowance of grain, should I ever be able to relish it?"

"The man to decide a cause with half a word," exclaimed the Master, "is Tsz-lu!"

Tsz-lu never let a night pass between promise and performance.

"In hearing causes, I am like other men," said the Master. "The great point is—to prevent litigation."

Tsz-chang having raised some question about government, the Master said to him, "In the settlement of its principles be unwearied; in its administration—see to that loyally."

"The man of wide research," said he, "who also restrains himself by the Rules of Propriety, is not likely to transgress."

Again, "The noble-minded man makes the most of others' good qualities, not the worst of their bad ones. Men of small mind do the reverse of this."

Ki K'ang was consulting him about the direction of public affairs. Confucius answered him, "A director should be himself correct. If you, sir, as a leader show correctness, who will dare not to be correct?"

Ki K'ang, being much troubled on account of robbers abroad, consulted Confucius on the matter. He received this reply: "If you, sir, were not covetous, neither would they steal, even were you to bribe them to do so."

Ki K'ang, when consulting Confucius about the government, said, "Suppose I were to put to death the disorderly for the better encouragement of the orderly—what say you to that?"

"Sir," replied Confucius, "in the administration of government why resort to capital punishment? Covet what is good, and the people will be good. The virtue of the noble-minded man is as the wind, and that of inferior men as grass; the grass must bend, when the wind blows upon it."

Tsz-chang asked how otherwise he would describe the learned official who might be termed influential.

"What, I wonder, do you mean by one who is influential?" said the Master.

"I mean," replied the disciple, "one who is sure to have a reputation throughout the country, as well as at home."

"That," said the Master, "is reputation, not influence. The influential man, then, if he be one who is genuinely straightforward and loves what is just and right, a discriminator of men's words, and an observer of their looks, and in honor careful to prefer others to himself—will certainly have influence, both throughout the country and at home. The man of mere reputation, on the other hand, who speciously affects philanthropy, though in his way of procedure he acts contrary to it, while yet quite evidently engrossed with that virtue—will certainly have reputation, both in the country and at home."

Fan Ch'i, strolling with him over the ground below the place of the rain-dance, said to him, "I venture to ask how to raise the standard of virtue, how to reform dissolute habits, and how to discern what is illusory?"

"Ah! a good question indeed!" he exclaimed. "Well, is not putting duty first, and success second, a way of raising the standard of virtue? And is not attacking the evil in one's self, and not the evil which is in others, a way of reforming dissolute habits? And as to illusions, is not one morning's fit of anger, causing a man to forget himself, and even involving in the consequences those who are near and dear to him—is not that an illusion?"

The same disciple asked him what was meant by "a right regard for one's fellow-creatures." He replied, "It is love to man."

Asked by him again what was meant by wisdom, he replied, "It is knowledge of man."

Fan Ch'i did not quite grasp his meaning.

The Master went on to say, "Lift up the straight, set aside the crooked, so can you make the crooked straight."

Fan Ch'i left him, and meeting with Tsz-hiá he said, "I had an interview just now with the Master, and I asked him what wisdom was. In his answer he said, 'Lift up the straight, set aside the crooked, and so can you make the crooked straight.' What was his meaning?"

"Ah! words rich in meaning, those," said the other. "When Shun was emperor, and was selecting his men from among the multitude, he 'lifted up' Káu-yáu; and men devoid of right feelings towards their kind went far away. And when T'ang was emperor, and chose out his men from the crowd, he 'lifted up' I-yin—with the same result."

Tsz-kung was consulting him about a friend. "Speak to him frankly, and respectfully," said the Master, "and gently lead him on. If you do not succeed, then stop; do not submit yourself to indignity."

The learned Tsang observed, "In the society of books the 'superior man' collects his friends; in the society of his friends he is furthering good-will among men."

BOOK XIII

Answers on the Art of Governing—Consistency

Tsz-LU was asking about government. "Lead the way in it," said the Master, "and work hard at it."

Requested to say more, he added, "And do not tire of it."

Chung-kung, on being made first minister to the Chief of the Ki family, consulted the Master about government, and to him he said, "Let the heads of offices be heads. Excuse small faults. Promote men of sagacity and talent."

"But," he asked, "how am I to know the sagacious and talented, before promoting them?"

"Promote those whom you do know," said the Master. "As to those of whom you are uncertain, will others omit to notice them?"

Tsz-lu said to the Master, "As the prince of Wei, sir, has been waiting for you to act for him in his government, what is it your intention to take in hand first?"

"One thing of necessity," he answered—"the rectification of terms."

"That!" exclaimed Tsz-lu. "How far away you are, sir! Why such rectification?"

"What a rustic you are, Tsz-lu!" rejoined the Master. "A gentleman would be a little reserved and reticent in matters which he does not understand. If terms be incorrect, language will be incongruous; and if language be incongruous, deeds will be imperfect. So, again, when deeds are imperfect, propriety and harmony cannot prevail, and when this is the case laws relating to crime will fail in their aim; and if these last so fail, the people will not

68

know where to set hand or foot. Hence, a man of superior mind, certain first of his terms, is fitted to speak; and being certain of what he says can proceed upon it. In the language of such a person there is nothing heedlessly irregular—and that is the sum of the matter."

Fan Ch'i requested that he might learn something of husbandry. "For that," said the Master, "I am not equal to an old husbandman." Might he then learn something of gardening? he asked. "I am not equal to an old gardener," was the reply.

"A man of little mind, that!" said the Master, when Fan Ch'i had gone out. "Let a man who is set over the people love propriety, and they will not presume to be disrespectful. Let him be a lover of righteousness, and they will not presume to be aught but submissive. Let him love faithfulness and truth, and they will not presume not to lend him their hearty assistance. Ah, if all this only were so, the people from all sides would come to such a one, carrying their children on their backs. What need to turn his hand to husbandry?

"Though a man," said he, "could hum through the Odes —the three hundred—yet should show himself unskilled when given some administrative work to do for his country; though he might know much of that other lore, yet if, when sent on a mission to any quarter, he could answer no question personally and unaided, what after all is he good for?

"Let a leader," said he, "show rectitude in his own personal character, and even without directions from him things will go well. If he be not personally upright, his directions will not be complied with."

Once he made the remark, "The governments of Lu and of Wei are in brotherhood."

Of King, a son of the Duke of Wei, he observed that "he managed his household matters well. On his coming into possession, he thought, 'What a strange conglomeration!'—Coming to possess a little more, it was, 'Strange, such a result!' And when he became wealthy, 'Strange, such elegance!'"

The Master was on a journey to Wei, and Yen Yu was driving him. "What multitudes of people!" he exclaimed. Yen Yu asked him, "Seeing they are so numerous, what more would you do for them?"

"Enrich them," replied the Master.

"And after enriching them, what more would you do for them?"

"Instruct them."

"Were any one of our princes to employ me," he said, "after a twelvemonth I might have made some tolerable progress; but give me three years, and my work should be done."

Again, "How true is that saying, 'Let good men have the management of a country for a century, and they would be adequate to cope with evil-doers, and thus do away with capital punishments.'"

Again, "Suppose the ruler to possess true kingly qualities, then surely after one generation there would be good-will among men."

Again, "Let a ruler but see to his own rectitude, and what trouble will he then have in the work before him? If he be unable to rectify himself, how is he to rectify others?"

Once when Yen Yu was leaving the Court, the Master accosted him. "Why so late?" he asked. "Busy with legislation," Yen replied. "The details of it," suggested the Master; "had it been legislation, I should have been there to hear it, even though I am not in office."

Duke Ting asked if there were one sentence which, if acted upon, might have the effect of making a country prosperous.

Confucius answered, "A sentence could hardly be supposed to do so much as that. But there is a proverb people use which says, 'To play the prince is hard, to play the minister not easy.' Assuming that it is understood that 'to play the prince is hard,' would it not be probable that with that one sentence the country should be made to prosper?"

"Is there, then," he asked, "one sentence which, if acted upon, would have the effect of ruining a country?"

Confucius again replied, "A sentence could hardly be supposed to do so much as that. But there is a proverb men have which says, 'Not gladly would I play the prince, unless my words were ne'er withstood.' Assuming that the words were good, and that none withstood them, would not that also be good? But assuming that they were not good, and yet none withstood them, would it not be probable that with that one saying he would work his country's ruin?"

When the Duke of Sheh consulted him about government, he replied, "Where the near are gratified, the war will follow."

When Tsz-hiá became governor of Kü-fu, and consulted him about government, he answered, "Do not wish for speedy results. Do not look at trivial advantages. If you wish for speedy results, they will not be far-reaching; and if you regard trivial advantages you will not successfully deal with important affairs."

The Duke of Sheh in a conversation with Confucius said, "There are some straightforward persons in my neighborhood. If a father has stolen a sheep, the son will give evidence against him."

"Straightforward people in my neighborhood are different from those," said Confucius. "The father will hold a thing secret on his son's behalf, and the son does the same for his father. They are on their way to becoming straightforward."

Fan Ch'i was asking him about duty to one's fellowmen. "Be courteous," he replied, "in your private sphere; be serious in any duty you take in hand to do; be lealhearted in your intercourse with others. Even though you were to go amongst the wild tribes, it would not be right for you to neglect these duties."

In answer to Tsz-kung, who asked, "how he would characterize one who could fitly be called 'learned official,'" the Master said, "He may be so-called who in his private life is affected with a sense of his own unworthiness, and who, when sent on a mission to any quarter of the empire, would not disgrace his prince's commands."

"May I presume," said his questioner, "to ask what sort you would put next to such?"

"Him who is spoken of by his kinsmen as a dutiful son, and whom the folks of his neighborhood call 'good brother.'"

"May I still venture to ask whom you would place next in order?"

"Such as are sure to be true to their word, and effective in their work—who are given to hammering, as it were, upon one note—of inferior calibre indeed, but fit enough, I think, to be ranked next."

"How would you describe those who are at present in the government service?"

"Ugh! mere peck and panier men!—not worth taking into the reckoning."

Once he remarked, "If I cannot get *via media* men to impart instruction to, then I must of course take the impetuous and undisciplined! The impetuous ones will at least go forward and lay hold on things; and the undisciplined have at least something in them which needs to be brought out."

"The Southerners," said he, "have the proverb, 'The man who sticks not to rule will never make a charm-worker or a medical man.' Good!—'Whoever is intermittent in his practise of virtue will live to be ashamed of it.' Without prognostication," he added, "that will indeed be so."

"The nobler-minded man," he remarked, "will be agreeable even when he disagrees; the small-minded man will agree and be disagreeable."

Tsz-kung was consulting him, and asked, "What say you of a person who was liked by all in his village?"

"That will scarcely do," he answered.

"What, then, if they all disliked him?"

"That, too," said he, "is scarcely enough. Better if he were liked by the good folk in the village, and disliked by the bad."

"The superior man," he once observed, "is easy to serve, but difficult to please. Try to please him by the adoption of wrong principles, and you will fail. Also, when such a one employs others, he uses them according to their capacity. The inferior man is, on the other hand, difficult to serve, but easy to please. Try to please him by the adoption of wrong principles, and you will succeed. And when he employs others he requires them to be fully prepared for everything."

Again, "The superior man can be high without being haughty. The inferior man can be haughty if not high."

"The firm, the unflinching, the plain and simple, the slow to speak," said he once, "are approximating towards their duty to their fellow-men."

Tsz-lu asked how he would characterize one who might fitly be called an educated gentleman. The master replied, "He who can properly be so-called will have in him a seriousness of purpose, a habit of controlling himself, and an agreeableness of manner: among his friends and associates the seriousness and the self-control, and among his brethren the agreeableness of manner."

"Let good and able men discipline the people for seven years," said the Master, "and after that they may do to go to war."

But, said he, "To lead an undisciplined people to war—that I call throwing them away."

BOOK XIV

Good and Bad Government—Miscellaneous Sayings

YUEN SZ asked what might be considered to bring shame on one.

"Pay," said the Master; "pay—ever looking to that, whether the country be well or badly governed."

"When imperiousness, boastfulness, resentments, and covetousness cease to prevail among the people, may it be considered that mutual good-will has been effected?" To this question the Master replied, "A hard thing overcome, it may be considered. But as to the mutual good-will—I cannot tell."

"Learned officials," said he, "who hanker after a home life, are not worthy of being esteemed as such."

Again, "In a country under good government, speak boldly, act boldly. When the land is ill-governed, though you act boldly, let your words be moderate."

Again, "Men of virtue will needs be men of words—will speak out—but men of words are not necessarily men of virtue. They who care for their fellow-men will needs be bold, but the bold may not necessarily be such as care for their fellow-men."

Nan-kung Kwoh, who was consulting Confucius, observed respecting I, the skilful archer, and Ngau, who could propel a boat on dry land, that neither of them died a natural death; while Yu and Tsih, who with their own hands had labored at husbandry, came to wield imperial sway.

The Master gave him no reply. But when the speaker

had gone out he exclaimed, "A superior man, that! A man who values virtue, that!"

"There have been noble-minded men," said he, "who yet were wanting in philanthropy; but never has there been a small-minded man who had philanthropy in him."

He asked, "Can any one refuse to toil for those he loves? Can any one refuse to exhort, who is true-hearted?"

Speaking of the preparation of Government Notifications in his day he said, "P'i would draw up a rough sketch of what was to be said; the Shishuh then looked it carefully through and put it into proper shape; Tsz-yu next, who was master of the ceremonial of State intercourse, improved and adorned its phrases; and Tsz-ch'an of Tung-li added his scholarly embellishments thereto."

To some one who asked his opinion of the last-named, he said, "He was a kind-hearted man." Asked what he thought of Tsz-si, he exclaimed, "Alas for him! alas for him!"—Asked again about Kwan Chung, his answer was, "As to him, he once seized the town of P'in with its three hundred families from the Chief of the Pih clan, who, afterwards reduced to living upon coarse rice, with all his teeth gone, never uttered a word of complaint."

"It is no light thing," said he, "to endure poverty uncomplainingly; and a difficult thing to bear wealth without becoming arrogant."

Respecting Mang Kung-ch'oh, he said that, while he was fitted for something better than the post of chief officer in the Cháu or Wei families, he was not competent to act as minister in small States like those of T'ang or Sieh.

Tsz-lu asked how he would describe a perfect man. He replied, "Let a man have the sagacity of Tsang Wu-chung, the freedom from covetousness of Kung-ch'oh, the boldness of Chwang of P'in, and the attainments in polite arts

of Yen Yu; and gift him further with the graces taught by
the 'Books of Rites' and 'Music'—then he may be considered a perfect man. But," said he, "what need of such
in these days? The man that may be regarded as perfect
now is the one who, seeing some advantage to himself, is
mindful of righteousness; who, seeing danger, risks his life;
and who, if bound by some covenant of long standing,
never forgets its conditions as life goes on."

Respecting Kung-shuh Wan, the Master inquired of
Kung-ming Kiá, saying, "Is it true that your master never
speaks, never laughs, never takes aught from others?"

"Those who told you that of him," said he, "have gone
too far. My master speaks when there is occasion to do so,
and men are not surfeited with his speaking. When there
is occasion to be merry too, he will laugh, but men have
never over much of his laughing. And whenever it is just
and right to take things from others, he will take them,
but never so as to allow men to think him burdensome."
"Is that the case with him?" said the Master. "Can it be
so?"

Respecting Tsang Wu-chung the Master said, "When
he sought from Lu the appointment of a successor to him,
and for this object held on to his possession of the fortified
city of Fang—if you say he was not then using constraint
towards his prince, I must refuse to believe it."

Duke Wan of Tsin he characterized as "artful but not
upright"; and Duke Hwan of Ts'i as "upright but not artful."

Tsz-lu remarked, "When Duke Hwan caused his brother
Kiu to be put to death, Shau Hwuh committed suicide,
but Kwan Chung did not. I should say he was not a man
who had much good-will in him—eh?"

The Master replied, "When Duke Hwan held a great
gathering of the feudal lords, dispensing with military

equipage, it was owing to Kwan Chung's energy that such an event was brought about. Match such good-will as that —match it if you can."

Tsz-kung then spoke up. "But was not Kwan Chung wanting in good-will? He could not give up his life when Duke Hwan caused his brother to be put to death. Besides, he became the duke's counsellor."

"And in acting as his counsellor put him at the head of all the feudal lords," said the Master, "and unified and reformed the whole empire; and the people, even to this day, reap benefit from what he did. Had it not been for him we should have been going about with locks unkempt and buttoning our jackets (like barbarians) on the left. Would you suppose that he should show the same sort of attachment as exists between a poor yokel and his one wife —that he would asphyxiate himself in some sewer, leaving no one the wiser?"

Kung-shuh Wan's steward, who became the high officer Sien, went up accompanied by Wan to the prince's hall of audience.

When Confucius heard of this he remarked, "He may well be esteemed a 'Wan.'"

The Master having made some reference to the lawless ways of Duke Ling of Wei, Ki K'ang said to him, "If he be like that, how is it he does not ruin his position?"

Confucius answered, "The Chung-shuh, Yu, is charged with the entertainment of visitors and strangers; the priest T'o has charge of the ancestral temple; and Wang-sun Kiá has the control of the army and its divisions:—with men such as those, how should he come to ruin?"

He once remarked, "He who is unblushing in his words will with difficulty substantiate them."

Ch'in Shing had slain Duke Kien. Hearing of this, Confucius, after performing his ablutions, went to Court and announced the news to Duke Ngai, saying, "Ch'in Shing has slain his prince. May I request that you proceed against him?"

"Inform the Chiefs of the Three Families," said the duke.

Soliloquizing upon this, Confucius said, "Since he uses me to back his ministers,[1] I did not dare not to announce the matter to him; and now he says, 'Inform the Three Chiefs.'"

He went to the Three Chiefs and informed them, but nothing could be done. Whereupon again he said, "Since he uses me to back his ministers, I did not dare not to announce the matter."

Tsz-lu was questioning him as to how he should serve his prince. "Deceive him not, but reprove him," he answered.

"The minds of superior men," he observed, "trend upwards; those of inferior men trend downwards."

Again, "Students of old fixed their eyes upon themselves: now they learn with their eyes upon others."

Kü Pih-yuh despatched a man with a message to Confucius. Confucius gave him a seat, and among other inquiries he asked, "How is your master managing?" "My master," he replied, "has a great wish to be seldom at fault, and as yet he cannot manage it."

"What a messenger!" exclaimed he, admiringly, when the man went out. "What a messenger!"

"When not occupying the office," was a remark of his, "devise not the policy."

The Learned Tsang used to say, "The thoughts of the 'superior man' do not wander from his own office."

"Superior men," said the Master, "are modest in their words, profuse in their deeds."

Again, "There are three attainments of the superior man

[1] Confucius had now retired from office, and this incident occurred only two years before his death.

which are beyond me—the being sympathetic without anxiety, wise without scepticism, brave without fear."

"Sir," said Tsz-kung, "that is what you say of yourself."

Whenever Tsz-kung drew comparisons from others, the Master would say, "Ah, how wise and great you must have become! Now I have no time to do that."

Again, "My great concern is, not that men do not know me, but that they cannot."

Again, "If a man refrain from making preparations against his being imposed upon, and from counting upon others' want of good faith towards him, while he is foremost to perceive what is passing—surely that is a wise and good man."

Wi-shang Mau accosted Confucius, saying, "Kiu, how comes it that you manage to go perching and roosting in this way? Is it not because you show yourself so smart a speaker, now?"

"I should not dare do that," said Confucius. " 'Tis that I am sick of men's immovableness and deafness to reason."

"In a well-bred horse," said he, "what one admires is not its speed, but its good points."

Some one asked, "What say you of the remark, 'Requite enmity with kindness'?"

"How then," he answered, "would you requite kindness? Requite enmity with straightforwardness, and kindness with kindness."

"Ah! no one knows me!" he once exclaimed.

"Sir," said Tsz-kung, "how comes it to pass that no one knows you?"

"While I murmur not against Heaven," continued the Master, "nor cavil at men; while I stoop to learn and aspire to penetrate into things that are high; yet 'tis Heaven alone knows what I am."

Liáu, a kinsman of the duke, having laid a complaint against Tsz-lu before Ki K'ang, an officer came to Confucius to inform him of the fact, and he added, "My lord is certainly having his mind poisoned by his kinsman Liáu, but through my influence perhaps we may yet manage to see him exposed in the market-place or the Court."

"If right principles are to have their course, it is so destined," said the Master; "if they are not to have their course, it is so destined. What can Liáu do against Destiny?"

"There are worthy men," said the Master, "fleeing from the world; some from their district; some from the sight of men's looks; some from the language they hear."

"The men who have risen from their posts and withdrawn in this manner are seven in number."

Tsz-lu, having lodged overnight in Shih-mun, was accosted by the gate-keeper in the morning. "Where from?" he asked. "From Confucius," Tsz-lu responded. "That is the man," said he, "who knows things are not up to the mark, and is making some ado about them, is it not?"

When the Master was in Wei, he was once pounding on the musical stone, when a man with a basket of straw crossed his threshold, and exclaimed, "Ah, there is a heart that feels! Aye, drub the stone!" After which he added, "How vulgar! how he hammers away on one note!—and no one knows him, and he gives up, and all is over!

'Be it deep, our skirts we'll raise to the waist,
—Or shallow, then up to the knee.' "

"What determination!" said the Master. "Yet it was not hard to do."

Tsz-chang once said to him, "In the 'Book of the Annals' it is stated that while Káu-tsung was in the Mourning Shed he spent the three years without speaking. What is meant by that?"

"Why must you name Káu-tsung?" said the Master. "It was so with all other ancient sovereigns: when one of them died, the heads of every department agreed between themselves that they should give ear for three years to the Prime Minister."

"When their betters love the Rules, then the folk are easy tools," was a saying of the Master.

Tsz-lu having asked what made a "superior man," he answered, "Self-culture, with a view to becoming seriously-minded."

"Nothing more than that?" said he.

"Self-culture with a view to the greater satisfaction of others," added the Master.

"That, and yet no more?"

"Self-culture with a view to the greater satisfaction of all the clans and classes," he again added. "Self-culture for the sake of all—a result that, that would almost put Yau and Shun into the shade!"

To Yuen Jang,[2] who was sitting waiting for him in a squatting (disrespectful) posture, the Master delivered himself as follows: "The man who in his youth could show no humility or subordination, who in his prime misses his opportunity, and who when old age comes upon him will not die—that man is a miscreant." And he tapped him on the shin with his staff.

Some one asked about his attendant—a youth from the village of Kiueh—whether he was one who improved. He replied, "I note that he seats himself in the places reserved for his betters, and that when he is walking he keeps abreast with his seniors. He is not one of those who care for improvement: he wants to be a man all at once."

[2] It is a habit with the Chinese, when a number are out walking together, for the eldest to go first, the others pairing off according to their age. It is a custom much older than the time of Confucius.

BOOK XV

Practical Wisdom—Reciprocity the Rule of Life

DUKE LING of Wei was consulting Confucius about army arrangements. His answer was, "Had you asked me about such things as temple requisites, I have learnt that business, but I have not yet studied military matters." And he followed up this reply by leaving on the following day.

After this, during his residence in the State of Ch'in, his followers, owing to a stoppage of food supply, became so weak and ill that not one of them could stand. Tsz-lu, with indignation pictured on his countenance, exclaimed, "And is a gentleman to suffer starvation?"

"A gentleman," replied the Master, "will endure it unmoved, but a common person breaks out into excesses under it."

Addressing Tsz-kung, the Master said, "You regard me as one who studies and stores up in his mind a multiplicity of things—do you not?"—"I do," he replied; "is it not so?" —"Not at all. I have one idea—one cord on which to string all."

To Tsz-lu he remarked, "They who know Virtue are rare."

"If you would know one who without effort ruled well, was not Shun such a one? What did he indeed do? He bore himself with reverent dignity and undeviatingly 'faced the south,' and that was all."

Tsz-chang was consulting him about making way in life. He answered, "Be true and honest in all you say, and seriously earnest in all you do, and then, even if your country be one inhabited by barbarians, South or North, you will make your way. If you do not show yourself thus in word and deed how should you succeed, even in your own district or neighborhood?—When you are afoot, let these two counsels be two companions preceding you, yourself viewing them from behind; when you drive, have them in view as on the yoke of your carriage. Then may you make your way."

Tsz-chang wrote them on the two ends of his cincture.

"Straight was the course of the Annalist Yu," said the Master—"aye, straight as an arrow flies; were the country well governed or ill governed, his was an arrow-like course.

"A man of masterly mind, too, is Kü Pih-yuh! When the land is being rightly governed he will serve; when it is under bad government he is apt to recoil, and brood."

"Not to speak to a man," said he, "to whom you ought to speak, is to lose your man; to speak to one to whom you ought not to speak is to lose your words. Those who are wise will not lose their man, nor yet their words."

Again, "The scholar whose heart is in his work, and who is philanthropic, seeks not to gain a livelihood by any means that will do harm to his philanthropy. There have been men who have destroyed their own lives in the endeavor to bring that virtue in them to perfection."

Tsz-kung asked how to become philanthropic. The Master answered him thus: "A workman who wants to do his work well must first sharpen his tools. In whatever land you live, serve under some wise and good man among those in high office, and make friends with the more humane of its men of education."

Yen Yuen consulted him on the management of a country. He answered:—

"Go by the Hiá Calendar. Have the State carriages like those of the Yin princes. Wear the Chow cap. For your

music let that of Shun be used for the posturers. Put away
the songs of Ch'ing, and remove far from you men of artful speech: the Ch'ing songs are immodest, and artful
talkers are dangerous."

Other sayings of the Master:—

"They who care not for the morrow will the sooner have
their sorrow.

"Ah, 'tis hopeless! I have not yet met with the man who
loves Virtue as he loves Beauty.

"Was not Tsang Wan like one who surreptitiously came
by the post he held? He knew the worth of Hwúi of Liu-
hiá, and could not stand in his presence.

"Be generous yourself, and exact little from others; then
you banish complaints.

"With one who does not come to me inquiring 'What of
this?' and 'What of that?' I never can ask 'What of this?'
and give him up.

"If a number of students are all day together, and in
their conversation never approach the subject of righteousness, but are fond merely of giving currency to smart
little sayings, they are difficult indeed to manage.

"When the 'superior man' regards righteousness as the
thing material, gives operation to it according to the Rules
of Propriety, lets it issue in humility, and become complete in sincerity—there indeed is your superior man!

"The trouble of the superior man will be his own want
of ability: it will be no trouble to him that others do not
know him.

"Such a man thinks it hard to end his days and leave a
name to be no longer named.

"The superior man is exacting of himself; the common
man is exacting of others.

"A superior man has self-respect, and does not strive; is
sociable, yet no party man.

"He does not promote a man because of his words, or pass over the words because of the man."

Tsz-kung put to him the question, "Is there one word upon which the whole life may proceed?"

The Master replied, "Is not Reciprocity such a word? —what you do not yourself desire, do not put before others."

"So far as I have to do with others, whom do I over-censure? whom do I over-praise? If there be something in them that looks very praiseworthy, that something I put to the test. I would have the men of the present day to walk in the straight path whereby those of the Three Dynasties have walked.

"I have arrived as it were at the annalist's blank page. —Once he who had a horse would lend it to another to mount; now, alas! it is not so.

"Artful speech is the confusion of Virtue. Impatience over little things introduces confusion into great schemes.

"What is disliked by the masses needs inquiring into; so also does that which they have a preference for.

"A man may give breadth to his principles: it is not principles (in themselves) that give breadth to the man.

"Not to retract after committing an error may itself be called error.

"If I have passed the whole day without food and the whole night without sleep, occupied with my thoughts, it profits me nothing: I were better engaged in learning.

"The superior man deliberates upon how he may walk in truth, not upon what he may eat. The farmer may plough, and be on the way to want: the student learns, and is on his way to emolument. To live a right life is the concern of men of nobler minds: poverty gives them none.

"Whatsoever the intellect may attain to, unless the humanity within is powerful enough to keep guard over it, is assuredly lost, even though it be gained.

"If there be intellectual attainments, and the humanity within is powerful enough to keep guard over them, yet, unless (in a ruler) there be dignity in his rule, the people will fail to show him respect.

"Again, given the intellectual attainments, and humanity sufficient to keep watch over them, and also dignity in ruling, yet if his movements be not in accordance with the Rules of Propriety, he is not yet fully qualified.

"The superior man may not be conversant with petty details, and yet may have important matters put into his hands. The inferior man may not be charged with important matters, yet may be conversant with the petty details.

"Good-fellowship is more to men than fire and water. I have seen men stepping into fire and into water, and meeting with death thereby; I have not yet seen a man die from planting his steps in the path of good-fellowship.

"Rely upon good nature. 'Twill not allow precedence even to a teacher.

"The superior man is inflexibly upright, and takes not things upon trust.

"In serving your prince, make your service the serious concern, and let salary be a secondary matter.

"Where instruction is to be given, there must be no distinction of persons.

"Where men's methods are not identical, there can be no planning by one on behalf of another.

"In speaking, perspicuity is all that is needed."

When the blind music-master Mien paid him a visit, on his approaching the steps the Master called out "Steps," and on his coming to the mat, said "Mat." When all in the room were seated, the Master told him "So-and-so is here, so-and-so is here."

When the music-master had left, Tsz-chang said to him, "Is that the way to speak to the music-master?" "Well," he replied, "it is certainly the way to assist him."

BOOK XVI

Against Intestine Strife—Good and Bad Friendships

THE Chief of the Ki family was about to make an onslaught upon the Chuen-yu domain.

Yen Yu and Tsz-lu in an interview with Confucius told him, "The Ki is about to have an affair with Chuen-yu."

"Yen," said Confucius, "does not the fault lie with you? The Chief of Chuen-yu in times past was appointed lord of the East Mung (mountain); besides, he dwells within the confines of your own State, and is an official of the State-worship; how can you think of making an onslaught upon him?"

"It is the wish of our Chief," said Yen Yu, "not the wish of either of us ministers."

Confucius said, "Yen, there is a sentence of Cháu Jin which runs thus: 'Having made manifest their powers and taken their place in the official list, when they find themselves incompetent they resign; if they cannot be firm when danger threatens the government, nor lend support when it is reeling, of what use then shall they be as Assistants?'—Besides, you are wrong in what you said. When a rhinoceros or tiger breaks out of its cage—when a jewel or tortoise-shell ornament is damaged in its casket—whose fault is it?"

"But," said Yen Yu, "so far as Chuen-yu is concerned, it is now fortified, and it is close to Pi; and if he does not now take it, in another generation it will certainly be a trouble to his descendants."

"Yen!" exclaimed Confucius, "it is a painful thing to a

superior man to have to desist from saying, 'My wish is so-and-so,' and to be obliged to make apologies. For my part, I have learnt this—that rulers of States and heads of Houses are not greatly concerned about their small following, but about the want of equilibrium in it—that they do not concern themselves about their becoming poor, but about the best means of living quietly and contentedly; for where equilibrium is preserved there will be no poverty, where there is harmony their following will not be small, and where there is quiet contentment there will be no decline nor fall. Now if that be the case, it follows that if men in outlying districts are not submissive, then a reform in education and morals will bring them to; and when they have been so won, then will you render them quiet and contented. At the present time you two are Assistants of your Chief; the people in the outlying districts are not submissive, and cannot be brought round. Your dominion is divided, prostrate, dispersed, cleft in pieces, and you as its guardians are powerless. And plans are being made for taking up arms against those who dwell within your own State. I am apprehensive that the sorrow of the Ki family is not to lie in Chuen-yu, but in those within their own screen."

"When the empire is well-ordered," said Confucius, "it is from the emperor that edicts regarding ceremonial, music, and expeditions to quell rebellion go forth. When it is being ill governed, such edicts emanate from the feudal lords; and when the latter is the case, it will be strange if in ten generations there is not a collapse. If they emanate merely from the high officials, it will be strange if the collapse do not come in five generations. When the State-edicts are in the hands of the subsidiary ministers, it will be strange if in three generations there is no collapse.

"When the empire is well-ordered, government is not left in the hands of high officials.

"When the empire is well-ordered, the common people will cease to discuss public matters."

"For five generations," he said, "the revenue has departed from the ducal household. Four generations ago the government fell into the hands of the high officials. Hence, alas! the straitened means of the descendants of the three Hwan families."

"There are," said he, "three kinds of friendships which are profitable, and three which are detrimental. To make friends with the upright, with the trustworthy, with the experienced, is to gain benefit; to make friends with the subtly perverse, with the artfully pliant, with the subtle in speech, is detrimental."

Again, "There are three kinds of pleasure which are profitable, and three which are detrimental. To take pleasure in going regularly through the various branches of Ceremonial and Music, in speaking of others' goodness, in having many worthy wise friends, is profitable. To take pleasure in wild bold pleasures, in idling carelessly about, in the too jovial accompaniments of feasting, is detrimental."

Again, "Three errors there be, into which they who wait upon their superior may fall:—(1) to speak before the opportunity comes to them to speak, which I call heedless haste; (2) refraining from speaking when the opportunity has come, which I call concealment; and (3) speaking, regardless of the mood he is in, which I call blindness."

Again, "Three things a superior should guard against:— (1) against the lusts of the flesh in his earlier years while the vital powers are not fully developed and fixed; (2) against the spirit of combativeness when he has come to the age of robust manhood and when the vital powers are matured and strong, and (3) against ambitiousness when old age has come on and the vital powers have become weak and decayed."

"Three things also such a man greatly reveres:—(1) the ordinances of Heaven, (2) great men, (3) words of sages. The inferior man knows not the ordinances of Heaven and therefore reveres them not, is unduly familiar in the presence of great men, and scoffs at the words of sages."

"They whose knowledge comes by birth are of all men the first in understanding; they to whom it comes by study are next; men of poor intelectual capacity, who yet study, may be added as a yet inferior class; and lowest of all are they who are poor in intellect and never learn."

"Nine things there are of which the superior man should be mindful:—to be clear in vision, quick in hearing, genial in expression, respectful in demeanor, true in word, serious in duty, inquiring in doubt, firmly self-controlled in anger, just and fair when the way to success opens out before him."

"Some have spoken of 'looking upon goodness as upon something beyond their reach,' and of 'looking upon evil as like plunging one's hands into scalding liquid';—I have seen the men, I have heard the sayings.

"Some, again, have talked of 'living in seclusion to work out their designs,' and of 'exercising themselves in righteous living in order to render their principles the more effective';—I have heard the sayings, I have not seen the men."

"Duke King of Ts'i had his thousand teams of four, yet on the day of his death the people had nothing to say of his goodness. Peh-I and Shuh-Ts'i starved at the foot of Shau-yang, and the people make mention of them to this day.

> 'E'en if not wealth thine object be,
> 'Tis all the same, thou'rt changed to me.'

"Is not this apropos in such cases?"

Tsz-k'in asked of Pih-yu, "Have you heard anything else peculiar from your father?"

"Not yet," said he. "Once, though, he was standing alone when I was hurrying past him over the vestibule, and he said, 'Are you studying the Odes?' 'Not yet,' I replied. 'If you do not learn the Odes,' said he, 'you will not have the wherewithal for conversing.' I turned away and studied the Odes. Another day, when he was again standing alone and I was hurrying past across the vestibule, he said to me, 'Are you learning the Rules of Propriety?' 'Not yet,' I replied. 'If you have not studied the Rules, you have nothing to stand upon,' said he. I turned away and studied the Rules.—These two things I have heard from him."

Tsz-k'in turned away, and in great glee exclaimed, "I asked one thing, and have got three. I have learnt something about the Odes, and about the Rules, and moreover I have learnt how the superior man will turn away his own son."

The wife of the ruler of a State is called by her husband "My helpmeet." She speaks of herself as "Your little handmaiden." The people of that State call her "The prince's helpmeet," but addressing persons of another State they speak of her as "Our little princess." When persons of another State name her they say also "Your prince's helpmeet."

BOOK XVII

The Master Induced to Take Office—Nature and Habit

YANG HO was desirous of having an interview with Confucius, but on the latter's failing to go and see him, he sent a present of a pig to his house. Confucius went to return his acknowledgments for it at a time when he was not at home. They met, however, on the way.

He said to Confucius, "Come, I want a word with you. Can that man be said to have good-will towards his fellow-men who hugs and hides his own precious gifts and allows his country to go on in blind error?"

"He cannot," was the reply.

"And can he be said to be wise who, with a liking for taking part in the public service, is constantly letting slip his opportunities?"

"He cannot," was the reply again.

"And the days and months are passing; and the years do not wait for us."

"True," said Confucius; "I will take office."

It was a remark of the Master that while "by nature we approximate towards each other, by experience we go far asunder."

Again, "Only the supremely wise and the most deeply ignorant do not alter."

The Master once, on his arrival at Wu-shing, heard the sound of stringed instruments and singing. His face beamed with pleasure, and he said laughingly, "To kill a cock—why use an ox-knife?"

Tsz-yu, the governor, replied, "In former days, sir, I

heard you say, 'Let the superior man learn right principles, and he will be loving to other men; let the ordinary person learn right principles, and he will be easily managed.'"

The Master (turning to his disciples) said, "Sirs, what he says is right: what I said just now was only in play."

Having received an invitation from Kung-shan Fuh-jau, who was in revolt against the government and was holding to his district of Pi, the Master showed an inclination to go.

Tsz-lu was averse to this, and said, "You can never go, that is certain; how should you feel you must go to that person?"

"Well," said the Master, "he who has invited me must surely not have done so without a sufficient reason! And if it should happen that my services were enlisted, I might create for him another East Chow—don't you think so?"

Tsz-chang asked Confucius about the virtue of philanthropy. His answer was, "It is the being able to put in practice five qualities, in any place under the sun."

"May I ask, please, what these are?" said the disciple.

"They are," he said, "dignity, indulgence, faithfulness, earnestness, kindness. If you show dignity you will not be mocked; if you are indulgent you will win the multitude; if faithful, men will place their trust in you; if earnest, you will do something meritorious; and if kind, you will be enabled to avail yourself amply of men's services."

Pih Hih sent the Master an invitation, and he showed an inclination to go.

Tsz-lu (seeing this) said to him, "In former days, sir, I have heard you say, 'A superior man will not enter the society of one who does not that which is good in matters concerning himself'; and this man is in revolt, with Chung-mau in his possession; if you go to him, how will the case stand?"

"Yes," said the Master, "those are indeed my words; but is it not said, 'What is hard may be rubbed without being made thin,' and 'White may be stained without being made black'?—I am surely not a gourd! How am I to be strung up like that kind of thing—and live without means?"

"Tsz-lu," said the Master, "you have heard of the six words with their six obfuscations?"

"No," said he, "not so far."

"Sit down, and I will tell you them. They are these six virtues, cared for without care for any study about them: —philanthropy, wisdom, faithfulness, straightforwardness, courage, firmness. And the six obfuscations resulting from not liking to learn about them are, respectively, these:— fatuity, mental dissipation, mischievousness, perversity, insubordination, impetuosity."

"My children," said he once, "why does no one of you study the Odes?—They are adapted to rouse the mind, to assist observation, to make people sociable, to arouse virtuous indignation. They speak of duties near and far—the duty of ministering to a parent, the duty of serving one's prince; and it is from them that one becomes conversant with the names of many birds, and beasts, and plants, and trees."

To his son Pih-yu he said, "Study you the Odes of Chow and the South, and those of Sháu and the South. The man who studies not these is, I should say, somewhat in the position of one who stands facing a wall!"

" 'Etiquette demands it.' 'Etiquette demands it,' so people plead," said he; "but do not these hankerings after jewels and silks indeed demand it? Or it is, 'The study of Music requires it'—'Music requires it'; but do not these predilections for bells and drums require it?"

Again, "They who assume an outward appearance of severity, being inwardly weak, may be likened to low common men; nay, are they not somewhat like thieves that break through walls and steal?"

Again, "The plebeian kind of respect for piety is the very pest of virtue."

Again, "Listening on the road, and repeating in the lane—this is abandonment of virtue."

"Ah, the low-minded creatures!" he exclaimed. "How is it possible indeed to serve one's prince in their company? Before they have got what they wanted they are all anxiety to get it, and after they have got it they are all anxiety lest they should lose it; and while they are thus full of concern lest they should lose it, there is no length to which they will not go."

Again, "In olden times people had three moral infirmities; which, it may be, are now unknown. Ambitiousness in those olden days showed itself in momentary outburst; the ambitiousness of to-day runs riot. Austerity in those days had its sharp angles; in these it is irritable and perverse. Feebleness of intellect then was at least straightforward; in our day it is never aught but deceitful."

Again, "Rarely do we find mutual good feeling where there is fine speech and studied mien."

Again, "To me it is abhorrent that purple color should be made to detract from that of vermilion. Also that the Odes of Ch'ing should be allowed to introduce discord in connection with the music of the Festal Songs and Hymns. Also that sharp-whetted tongues should be permitted to subvert governments."

Once said he, "Would that I could dispense with speech!"

"Sir," said Tsz-kung, "if you were never to speak, what should your pupils have to hand down from you?"

"Does Heaven ever speak?" said the Master. "The four seasons come and go, and all creatures live and grow. Does Heaven indeed speak?"

Once Ju Pi desired an interview with Confucius, from

which the latter excused himself on the score of ill-health; but while the attendant was passing out through the doorway with the message he took his lute and sang, in such a way as to let him hear him.

Tsai Wo questioned him respecting the three years' mourning, saying that one full twelve-month was a long time—that, if gentlemen were for three years to cease from observing rules of propriety, propriety must certainly suffer, and that if for three years they neglected music, music must certainly die out—and that seeing nature has taught us that when the old year's grain is finished the new has sprung up for us—seeing also that all the changes[1] in procuring fire by friction have been gone through in the four seasons—surely a twelve-month might suffice.

The Master asked him, "Would it be a satisfaction to you—that returning to better food, that putting on of fine clothes?"

"It would," said he.

"Then if you can be satisfied in so doing, do so. But to a gentleman, who is in mourning for a parent, the choicest food will not be palatable, nor will the listening to music be pleasant, nor will comforts of home make him happy in mind. Hence he does not do as you suggest. But if you are now happy in your mind, then do so."

Tsai Wo went out. And the Master went on to say, "It is want of human feeling in this man. After a child has lived three years it then breaks away from the tender nursing of its parents. And this three years' mourning is the customary mourning prevalent all over the empire. Can this man have enjoyed the three years of loving care from his parents?"

"Ah, it is difficult," said he, "to know what to make of those who are all day long cramming themselves with food

[1] Different woods were adopted for this purpose at the various seasons.

and are without anything to apply their minds to! Are there no dice and chess players? Better, perhaps, join in that pursuit than do nothing at all!"

"Does a gentleman," asked Tsz-lu, "make much account of bravery?"

"Righteousness he counts higher," said the Master. "A gentleman who is brave without being just may become turbulent; while a common person who is brave and not just may end in becoming a highwayman."

Tsz-kung asked, "I suppose a gentleman will have his aversions as well as his likings?"

"Yes," replied the Master, "he will dislike those who talk much about other people's ill-deeds. He will dislike those who, when occupying inferior places, utter defamatory words against their superiors. He will dislike those who, though they may be brave, have no regard for propriety. And he will dislike those hastily decisive and venturesome spirits who are nevertheless so hampered by limited intellect."

"And you, too, Tsz-kung," he continued, "have your aversions, have you not?"

"I dislike," said he, "those plagiarists who wish to pass for wise persons. I dislike those people who wish their lack of humility to be taken for bravery. I dislike also those divulgers of secrets who think to be accounted straightforward."

"Of all others," said the Master, "women-servants and men-servants are the most difficult people to have the care of. Approach them in a familiar manner, and they take liberties; keep them at a distance, and they grumble."

Again, "When a man meets with odium at forty, he will do so to the end."

BOOK XVIII

Good Men in Seclusion—Duke of Chow to His Son

"In the reign of the last king of the Yin dynasty," Confucius said, "there were three men of philanthropic spirit: —the viscount of Wei, who withdrew from him; the viscount of Ki, who became his bondsman; and Pi-kan, who reproved him and suffered death."

"Hwúi of Liu-hiá, who filled the office of Chief Criminal Judge, was thrice dismissed. A person remarked to him, "Can you not yet bear to withdraw?" He replied, "If I act in a straightforward way in serving men, whither in these days should I go, where I should not be thrice dismissed? Were I to adopt crooked ways in their service, why need I leave the land where my parents dwell?"

Duke King of Ts'i remarked respecting his attitude towards Confucius, "If he is to be treated like the Chief of the Ki family, I cannot do it. I should treat him as somewhere between the Ki and Mang Chiefs.—I am old," he added, "and not competent to avail myself of him."

Confucius, hearing of this, went away.

The Ts'i officials presented to the Court of Lu a number of female musicians. Ki Hwan accepted them, and for three days no Court was held.

Confucius went away.

Tsieh-yu, the madman[1] of Ts'u, was once passing Confucius, singing as he went along. He sang—

[1] He only pretended to be mad, in order to escape being employed in the public service.

"Ha, the phœnix! Ha, the phœnix!
How is Virtue lying prone!
Vain to chide for what is o'er,
Plan to meet what's yet in store.
Let alone! Let alone!
Risky now to serve a throne."

Confucius alighted, wishing to enter into conversation with him; but the man hurried along and left him, and he was therefore unable to get a word with him.

Ch'ang-tsü and Kieh-nih[2] were working together on some ploughed land. Confucius was passing by them, and sent Tsz-lu to ask where the ford was.

Ch'ang-tsü said, "Who is the person driving the carriage?"

"Confucius," answered Tsz-lu.

"He of Lu?" he asked.

"The same," said Tsz-lu.

"He knows then where the ford is," said he.

Tsz-lu then put his question to Kieh-nih; and the latter asked, "Who are you?"

Tsz-lu gave his name.

"You are a follower of Confucius of Lu, are you not?"

"You are right," he answered.

"Ah, as these waters rise and overflow their bounds," said he, "'tis so with all throughout the empire; and who is he that can alter the state of things? And you are a follower of a learned man who withdraws from his chief; had you not better be a follower of such as have forsaken the world?" And he went on with his harrowing, without stopping.

Tsz-lu went and informed his Master of all this. He was deeply touched, and said, "One cannot herd on equal terms with beasts and birds: if I am not to live among these human folk, then with whom else should I live? Only when

---

[2] Two worthies who had abandoned public life, owing to the state of the times.

the empire is well ordered shall I cease to take part in the work of reformation."

Tsz-lu was following the Master, but had dropped behind on the way, when he encountered an old man with a weed-basket slung on a staff over his shoulder. Tsz-lu inquired of him, "Have you seen my Master, sir?" Said the old man, "Who is your master?—you who never employ your four limbs in laborious work; you who do not know one from another of the five sorts of grain!" And he stuck his staff in the ground, and began his weeding.

Tsz-lu brought his hands together on his breast and stood still.

The old man kept Tsz-lu and lodged him for the night, killed a fowl and prepared some millet, entertained him, and brought his two sons out to see him.

On the morrow Tsz-lu went on his way, and told all this to the Master, who said, "He is a recluse," and sent Tsz-lu back to see him again. But by the time he got there he was gone.

Tsz-lu remarked upon this, "It is not right he should evade official duties. If he cannot allow any neglect of the terms on which elders and juniors should live together, how is it that he neglects to conform to what is proper as between prince and public servant? He wishes for himself personally a pure life, yet creates disorder in that more important relationship. When a gentleman undertakes public work, he will carry out the duties proper to it; and he knows beforehand that right principles may not win their way."

Among those who have retired from public life have been Peh-I and Shuh-Ts'i, Yu-chung, I-yih, Chu-chang, Hwúi of Liu-hiá, and Sháu-lien.

"Of these," said the Master, "Peh-I and Shuh-Ts'i may be characterized, I should say, as men who never declined from their high resolve nor soiled themselves by aught of disgrace.

"Of Hwúi of Liu-hiá and Sháu-lien, if one may say that they did decline from high resolve, and that they did bring disgrace upon themselves, yet their words were consonant with established principles, and their action consonant with men's thoughts and wishes; and this is all that may be said of them.

"Of Yu-chung and I-yih, if it be said that when they retired into privacy they let loose their tongues, yet in their aim at personal purity of life they succeeded, and their defection was also successful in its influence.

"My own rule is different from any adopted by these: I will take no liberties, I will have no curtailing of my liberty."

The chief music-master went off to Ts'i. Kan, the conductor of the music at the second repast, went over to Ts'u. Liáu, conductor at the third repast, went over to Ts'ai. And Kiueh, who conducted at the fourth, went to Ts'in.

Fang-shuh, the drummer, withdrew into the neighborhood of the Ho. Wu the tambourer went to the Han. And Yang the junior music-master, and Siang who played on the musical stone, went to the sea-coast.

Anciently the Duke of Chow, addressing his son the Duke of Lu, said, "A good man in high place is not indifferent about the members of his own family, and does not give occasion to the chief ministers to complain that they are not employed; nor without great cause will he set aside old friendships; nor does he seek for full equipment for every kind of service in any single man."

There were once eight officials during this Chow dynasty, who were four pairs of twins, all brothers—the eldest pair Tah and Kwoh, the next Tuh and Hwuh, the third Yé and Hiá, the youngest Sui and Kwa.

BOOK XIX

Teachings of Various Chief Disciples

"THE learned official," said Tsz-chang, "who when he sees danger ahead will risk his very life, who when he sees a chance of success is mindful of what is just and proper, who in his religious acts is mindful of the duty of reverence, and when in mourning thinks of his loss, is indeed a fit and proper person for his place."

Again he said, "If a person hold to virtue but never advance in it, and if he have faith in right principles and do not build himself up in them, how can he be regarded either as having such, or as being without them?"

Tsz-hiá's disciples asked Tsz-chang his views about intercourse with others. "What says your Master?" he rejoined. "He says," they replied, " 'Associate with those who are qualified, and repel from you such as are not.' " Tsz-chang then said, "That is different from what I have learnt. A superior man esteems the worthy and wise, and bears with all. He makes much of the good and capable, and pities the incapable. Am I eminently worthy and wise?—who is there then among men whom I will not bear with? Am I not worthy and wise?—others will be minded to repel me: I have nothing to do with repelling them."

Sayings of Tsz-hiá:—

"Even in inferior pursuits there must be something worthy of contemplation, but if carried to an extreme there is danger of fanaticism; hence the superior man does not engage in them.

"The student who daily recognizes how much he yet

lacks, and as the months pass forgets not what he has succeeded in learning, may undoubtedly be called a lover of learning.

"Wide research and steadfast purpose, eager questioning and close reflection—all this tends to humanize a man.

"As workmen spend their time in their workshops for the perfecting of their work, so superior men apply their minds to study in order to make themselves thoroughly conversant with their subjects.

"When an inferior man does a wrong thing, he is sure to gloss it over.

"The superior man is seen in three different aspects:—look at him from a distance, he is imposing in appearance; approach him, he is gentle and warm-hearted; hear him speak, he is acute and strict.

"Let such a man have the people's confidence, and he will get much work out of them; so long, however, as he does not possess their confidence they will regard him as grinding them down.

"When confidence is reposed in him, he may then with impunity administer reproof; so long as it is not, he will be regarded as a detractor.

"Where there is no over-stepping of barriers in the practice of the higher virtues, there may be freedom to pass in and out in the practice of the lower ones."

Tsz-yu had said, "The pupils in the school of Tsz-hiá are good enough at such things as sprinkling and scrubbing floors, answering calls and replying to questions from superiors, and advancing and retiring to and from such; but these things are only offshoots—as to the root of things they are nowhere. What is the use of all that?"

When this came to the ears of Tsz-hiá, he said, "Ah! there he is mistaken. What does a master, in his methods of teaching, consider first in his precepts? And what does he account next, as that about which he may be indifferent? It is like as in the study of plants—classification by *differentiæ*. How may a master play fast and loose in his methods of instruction? Would they not indeed be sages, who could take in at once the first principles and the final developments of things?"

Further observations of Tsz-hiá:—

"In the public service devote what energy and time remain to study. After study devote what energy and time remain to the public service.

"As to the duties of mourning, let them cease when the grief is past.

"My friend Tsz-chang, although he has the ability to tackle hard things, has not yet the virtue of philanthropy."

The learned Tsang observed, "How loftily Tsz-chang bears himself! Difficult indeed along with him to practise philanthropy!"

Again he said, "I have heard this said by the Master, that 'though men may not exert themselves to the utmost in other duties, yet surely in the duty of mourning for their parents they will do so!'"

Again, "This also I have heard said by the Master: 'The filial piety of Mang Chwang in other respects might be equalled, but as manifested in his making no changes among his father's ministers, nor in his father's mode of government—that aspect of it could not easily be equalled.'"

Yang Fu, having been made senior Criminal Judge by the Chief of the Mang clan, consulted with the learned Tsang. The latter advised him as follows: "For a long time the Chiefs have failed in their government, and the people have become unsettled. When you arrive at the facts of their cases, do not rejoice at your success in that, but rather be sorry for them, and have pity upon them."

Tsz-kung once observed, "We speak of 'the iniquity of Cháu'—but 'twas not so great as this." And so it is that the superior man is averse from settling in this sink, into which everything runs that is foul in the empire."

Again he said, "Faults in a superior man are like eclipses of the sun or moon: when he is guilty of a trespass men all see it; and when he is himself again, all look up to him."

Kung-sun Ch'au of Wei inquired of Tsz-kung how Confucius acquired his learning.

Tsz-kung replied, "The teachings of Wan and Wu have not yet fallen to the ground. They exist in men. Worthy and wise men have the more important of these stored up in their minds; and others, who are not such, store up the less important of them; and as no one is thus without the teachings of Wan and Wu, how should our Master not have learned? And moreover what permanent preceptor could he have?"

Shuh-sun Wu-shuh, addressing the high officials at the Court, remarked that Tsz-kung was a greater worthy than Confucius.

Tsz-fuh King-pih went and informed Tsz-kung of this remark.

Tsz-kung said, "Take by way of comparison the walls outside our houses. My wall is shoulder-high, and you may look over it and see what the house and its contents are worth. My Master's wall is tens of feet high, and unless you should effect an entrance by the door, you would fail to behold the beauty of the ancestral hall and the rich array of all its officers. And they who effect an entrance by the door, methinks, are few! Was it not, however, just like him —that remark of the Chief?"

Shuh-sun Wu-shuh had been casting a slur on the character of Confucius.

"No use doing that," said Tsz-kung; "he is irreproachable. The wisdom and worth of other men are little hills and mounds of earth: traversible. He is the sun, or the moon, impossible to reach and pass. And what harm, I ask,

can a man do to the sun or the moon, by wishing to intercept himself from either? It all shows that he knows not
how to gauge capacity."

Tsz-k'in, addressing Tsz-kung, said, "You depreciate
yourself. Confucius is surely not a greater worthy than
yourself."

Tsz-kung replied, "In the use of words one ought never
to be incautious; because a gentleman for one single utterance of his is apt to be considered a wise man, and for a
single utterance may be accounted unwise. No more might
one think of attaining to the Master's perfections than
think of going upstairs to Heaven! Were it ever his fortune to be at the head of the government of a country,
then that which is spoken of as 'establishing the country'
would be establishment indeed; he would be its guide and
it would follow him, he would tranquillize it and it would
render its willing homage: he would give forward impulses
to it to which it would harmoniously respond. In his life he
would be its glory, at his death there would be great lam-
entation. How indeed could such as he be equalled?"

BOOK XX

Extracts from the Book of History

THE Emperor Yau said to Shun, "Ah, upon you, upon your person, lies the Heaven-appointed order of succession! Faithfully hold to it, without any deflection; for if within the four seas necessity and want befall the people, your own revenue will forever come to an end."

Shun also used the same language in handing down the appointment to Yu.

The Emperor T'ang in his prayer, said, "I, the child Li, presume to avail me of an ox of dusky hue, and presume to manifestly announce to Thee, O God, the most high and Sovereign Potentate, that to the transgressor I dare not grant forgiveness, nor yet keep in abeyance Thy ministers. Judgment rests in Thine heart, O God. Should we ourself transgress, may the guilt not be visited everywhere upon all. Should the people all transgress, be the guilt upon ourself!"

Chow possessed great gifts, by which the able and good were richly endowed.

"Although," said King Wu, "he is surrounded by his near relatives, they are not to be compared with men of humane spirit. The people are suffering wrongs, and the remedy rests with me—the one man."

After Wu had given diligent attention to the various weights and measures, examined the laws and regulations, and restored the degraded officials, good government everywhere ensued.

He caused ruined States to flourish again, reinstated intercepted heirs, and promoted to office men who had gone into retirement; and the hearts of the people throughout the empire drew towards him.

Among matters of prime consideration with him were these—food for the people, the duty of mourning, and sacrificial offerings to the departed.

He was liberal and large-hearted, and so won all hearts; true, and so was trusted by the people; energetic, and thus became a man of great achievements; just in his rule, and all were well content.

Tsz-chang in a conversation with Confucius asked, "What say you is essential for the proper conduct of government?"

The Master replied, "Let the ruler hold in high estimation the five excellences, and eschew the four evils; then may he conduct his government properly."

"And what call you the five excellences?" he was asked.

"They are," he said, "bounty without extravagance; burdening without exciting discontent; desire without covetousness; dignity without haughtiness; show of majesty without fierceness."

"What mean you," asked Tsz-chang, "by bounty without extravagance?"

"Is it not this," he replied—"to make that which is of benefit to the people still more beneficial? When he selects for them such labors as it is possible for them to do, and exacts them, who will then complain? So when his desire is the virtue of humaneness, and he attains it, how shall he then be covetous? And if—whether he have to do with few or with many, with small or with great—he do not venture ever to be careless, is not this also to have dignity without haughtiness? And if—when properly vested in robe and cap, and showing dignity in his every look—his appearance be so imposing that the people look up to and stand in awe of him, is not this moreover to show majesty without fierceness?"

"What, then, do you call the four evils?" said Tsz-chang.

The answer here was, "Omitting to instruct the people and then inflicting capital punishment on them—which means cruel tyranny. Omitting to give them warning and yet looking for perfection in them—which means oppression. Being slow and late in issuing requisitions, and exacting strict punctuality in the returns—which means robbery. And likewise, in intercourse with men, to expend and to receive in a stingy manner—which is to act the part of a mere commissioner."

"None can be a superior man," said the Master, "who does not recognize the decrees of Heaven.

"None can have stability in him without a knowledge of the proprieties.

"None can know a man without knowing his utterances."

THE SAYINGS
OF MENCIUS

[Translated into English by James Legge]

INTRODUCTION

A HUNDRED years after the time of Confucius the Chinese nation seemed to have fallen back into their original condition of lawlessness and oppression. The King's power and authority was laughed to scorn, the people were pillaged by the feudal nobility, and famine reigned in many districts. The foundations of truth and social order seemed to be overthrown. There were teachers of immorality abroad, who published the old Epicurean doctrine, "Let us eat and drink, for to-morrow we die." This teaching was accompanied by a spirit of cold-blooded egotism which extinguished every spark of Confucian altruism. Even the pretended disciples of Confucius confused the precepts of the Master, and by stripping them of their narrow significance rendered them nugatory. It was at this point that Mang-tsze, "Mang the philosopher," arose. He was sturdy in bodily frame, vigorous in mind, profound in political sagacity and utterly fearless in denouncing the errors of his countrymen. He had been brought up among the disciples of Confucius, in whose province he was born B.C. 372, but he was much more active and aggressive, less a Mystic than a fanatic, in comparison with his Master. He resolved on active measures in stemming the tendency of his day. He did indeed surround himself with a school of disciples, but instead of making a series of desultory travels, teaching in remote places and along the high-road, he went to the heart of the evil. He presented himself like a second John the Baptist at the courts of kings and princes, and there boldly denounced vice and misrule. It was not difficult for a Chinese scholar and teacher to find

113

access to the highest of the land. The Chinese believed in
the divine right of learning, just as they believed in the
divine right of kings. Mang employed every weapon of
persuasion in trying to combat heresy and oppression;
alternately ridiculing and reproving: now appealing in a
burst of moral enthusiasm, and now denouncing in terms
of cutting sarcasm the abuses which after all he failed to
check. The last prince whom he successfully confronted
was the Marquis of Lu, who turned him carelessly away.
He accepted this as the Divine sentence of his failure,
"That I have not found in this marquis, a ruler who would
hearken to me is an intimation of heaven." Henceforth he
lived in retirement until his ninety-seventh year; but from
his apparent failure sprang a practical success. His written
teachings are amongst the most lively and epigrammatic
works of Chinese literature, have done much to keep alive
amongst his countrymen the spirit of Confucianism, and
even Western readers may drink wisdom from this spring
of Oriental lore. The following selections from his sayings
well exhibit the spirit of his system of philosophy and
morality: E. W.

BOOK I

King Hwuy of Lëang

PART I

Mencius went to see King Hwuy of Lëang.[1] The king said, "Venerable Sir, since you have not counted it far to come here a distance of a thousand li, may I presume that you are likewise provided with counsels to profit my kingdom?" Mencius replied, "Why must your Majesty use that word 'profit'? What I am likewise provided with are counsels to benevolence and righteousness; and these are my only topics.

"If your Majesty say, 'What is to be done to profit my kingdom?' the great officers will say, 'What is to be done to profit our families?' and the inferior officers and the common people will say, 'What is to be done to profit our persons?' Superiors and inferiors will try to take the profit the one from the other, and the kingdom will be endangered. In the kingdom of ten thousand chariots, the murderer of his ruler will be the chief of a family of a thousand chariots. In the State of a thousand chariots, the murderer of his ruler will be the chief of a family of a hundred chariots. To have a thousand in ten thousand, and a hundred in a thousand, cannot be regarded as not a large al-

---

[1] The title of this book in Chinese is—"King Hwuy of Lëang; in chapters and sentences." Like the Books of the Confucian Analects, those of this work are headed by two or three words at or near the commencement of them. Each Book is divided into two parts. This arrangement was made by Chaou K'e, and to him are due also the divisions into chapters, and sentences, or paragraphs, containing, it may be, many sentences.

115

lowance; but if righteousness be put last and profit first, they will not be satisfied without snatching all.

"There never was a man trained to benevolence who neglected his parents. There never was a man trained to righteousness who made his ruler an after consideration. Let your Majesty likewise make benevolence and right-eousness your only themes—Why must you speak of profit?"

When Mencius, another day, was seeing King Hwuy of Lëang, the King went and stood with him by a pond, and, looking round on the wild geese and deer, large and small, said, "Do wise and good princes also take pleasure in these things?" Mencius replied, "Being wise and good, they then have pleasure in these things. If they are not wise and good, though they have these things, they do not find pleasure." It is said in the 'Book of Poetry':—

When he planned the commencement of the Marvellous tower,
He planned it, and defined it,
And the people in crowds undertook the work,
And in no time completed it.
When he planned the commencement, he said, "Be not in a hurry."
But the people came as if they were his children.
The king was in the Marvellous park,
Where the does were lying down—
The does so sleek and fat;
With the white birds glistening.
The king was by the Marvellous pond;—
How full was it of fishes leaping about!'

King Wan used the strength of the people to make his tower and pond, and the people rejoiced to do the work, calling the tower 'the Marvellous Tower,' and the pond 'the Marvellous Pond,' and being glad that he had his deer, his fishes and turtles. The ancients caused their people to have pleasure as well as themselves, and therefore they could enjoy it.

"In the Declaration of T'ang it is said, 'O Sun, when wilt

thou expire? We will die together with thee.' The people wished for Këeh's death, though they should die with him. Although he had his tower, his pond, birds and animals, how could he have pleasure alone?"

King Hwuy of Lëang said, "Small as my virtue is, in the government of my kingdom, I do indeed exert my mind to the utmost. If the year be bad inside the Ho, I remove as many of the people as I can to the east of it, and convey grain to the country inside. If the year be bad on the east of the river, I act on the same plan. On examining the governmental methods of the neighboring kingdoms, I do not find there is any ruler who exerts his mind as I do. And yet the people of the neighboring kings do not decrease, nor do my people increase—how is this?"

Mencius replied, "Your Majesty loves war; allow me to take an illustration from war. The soldiers move forward at the sound of the drum; and when the edges of their weapons have been crossed, on one side, they throw away their buff coats, trail their weapons behind them, and run. Some run a hundred paces and then stop; some run fifty paces and stop. What would you think if these, because they had run but fifty paces, should laugh at those who ran a hundred paces?" The king said, "They cannot do so. They only did not run a hundred paces; but they also ran." Mencius said, "Since your Majesty knows this you have no ground to expect that your people will become more numerous than those of the neighboring kingdoms.

"If the seasons of husbandry be not interfered with, the grain will be more than can be eaten. If close nets are not allowed to enter the pools and ponds, the fish and turtles will be more than can be consumed. If the axes and bills enter the hill-forests only at the proper times, the wood will be more than can be used. When the grain and fish and turtles are more than can be eaten, and there is more wood than can be used, this enables the people to nourish their living and do all offices for their dead, without any feeling against any. But this condition, in which the people nourish their living, and do all offices to their dead without having any feeling against any, is the first step in the Royal way.

"Let mulberry trees be planted about the homesteads with their five acres, and persons of fifty years will be able to wear silk. In keeping fowls, pigs, dogs, and swine, let not their time of breeding be neglected, and persons of seventy years will be able to eat flesh. Let there not be taken away the time that is proper for the cultivation of the field allotment of a hundred acres, and the family of several mouths will not suffer from hunger. Let careful attention be paid to the teaching in the various schools, with repeated inculcation of the filial and fraternal duties, and gray-haired men will not be seen upon the roads, carrying burdens on their backs or on their heads. It has never been that the ruler of a State where these results were seen, persons of seventy wearing silk and eating flesh, and the black-haired people suffering neither from hunger nor cold, did not attain to the Royal dignity.

"Your dogs and swine eat the food of men, and you do not know to store up of the abundance. There are people dying from famine on the roads, and you do not know to issue your stores for their relief. When men die, you say, 'It is not owing to me; it is owing to the year.' In what does this differ from stabbing a man and killing him, and then saying, 'It was not I; it was the weapon'? Let your Majesty cease to lay the blame on the year and instantly the people, all under the sky, will come to you."

King Hwuy of Lëang said, "I wish quietly to receive your instructions." Mencius replied, "Is there any difference between killing a man with a stick and with a sword?" "There is no difference," was the answer.

Mencius continued, "Is there any difference between doing it with a sword and with governmental measures?" "There is not," was the answer again.

Mencius then said, "In your stalls there are fat beasts; in your stables there are fat horses. But your people have the look of hunger, and in the fields there are those who have died of famine. This is leading on beasts to devour men. Beasts devour one another, and men hate them for doing so. When he who is called the parent of the people conducts his government so as to be chargeable with leading on beasts to devour men, where is that parental relation to the people? Chung-ne said, 'Was he not without posterity who first made wooden images to bury with the dead?' So he said, because that man made the semblances of men and used them for that purpose; what shall be thought of him who causes his people to die of hunger?"

King Hwuy of Lëang said, "There was not in the kingdom a stronger State than Ts'in, as you, venerable Sir, know. But since it descended to me, on the east we were defeated by Ts'e, and then my eldest son perished; on the west we lost seven hundred li of territory to Ts'in; and on the south we have sustained disgrace at the hands of Ts'oo. I have brought shame on my departed predecessors, and wish on their account to wipe it away once for all. What course is to be pursued to accomplish this?"

Mencius replied, "With a territory only a hundred li square it has been possible to obtain the Royal dignity. If your Majesty will indeed dispense a benevolent government to the people, being sparing in the use of punishments and fines, and making the taxes and levies of produce light, so causing that the fields shall be ploughed deep, and the weeding well attended to, and that the able-bodied, during their days of leisure, shall cultivate their filial piety, fraternal duty, faithfulness, and truth, serving thereby, at home, their fathers and elder brothers, and, abroad, their elders and superiors, you will then have a people who can be employed with sticks which they have prepared to oppose the strong buff-coats and sharp weapons of the troops of Ts'in and Ts'oo.

"The rulers of those States rob their people of their time, so that they cannot plough and weed their fields in order to support their parents. Parents suffer from cold and hunger; elder and younger brothers, wives and children, are separated and scattered abroad. Those rulers drive their people into pitfalls or into the water; and your Majesty will go to punish them. In such a case, who will oppose your Majesty? In accordance with this is the saying, 'The benevolent has no enemy!' I beg your Majesty not to doubt what I said."

Mencius had an interview with King Sëang[2] of Lëang. When he came out he said to some persons, "When I looked at him from a distance, he did not appear like a ruler; when I drew near to him, I saw nothing venerable about him. Abruptly he asked me, 'How can the kingdom, all under the sky, be settled?' I replied, 'It will be settled by being united under one sway.'

" 'Who can so unite it?' he asked.

"I replied, 'He who has no pleasure in killing men can so unite it.'

" 'Who can give it to him?' he asked.

"I replied, 'All under heaven will give it to him. Does your Majesty know the way of the growing grain? During the seventh and eighth months, when drought prevails, the plants become dry. Then the clouds collect densely in

[2] Sëang was the son of King Hwuy. The first year of his reign is supposed to be B.C. 317. Sëang's name was Hih. As a posthumous epithet, Sëang has various meanings: "Land-enlarger and Virtuous"; "Successful in Arms." The interview here recorded seems to have taken place immediately after Hih's accession, and Mencius, it is said, was so disappointed by it that he soon after left the country.

the heavens, and send down torrents of rain, so that the grain erects itself as if by a shoot. When it does so, who can keep it back? Now among those who are shepherds of men throughout the kingdom, there is not one who does not find pleasure in killing men. If there were one who did not find pleasure in killing men, all the people under the sky would be looking towards him with outstretched necks. Such being indeed the case, the people would go to him as water flows downwards with a rush, which no one can repress."

King Seuen of Ts'e asked, saying, "May I be informed by you of the transactions of Hwan of Ts'e and Wan of Ts'in?"

Mencius replied, "There were none of the disciples of Chung-ne who spoke about the affairs of Hwan and Wan, and therefore they have not been transmitted to these after-ages; your servant has not heard of them. If you will have me speak, let it be about the principles of attaining to the Royal sway."

The king said, "Of what kind must his virtue be who can attain to the Royal sway?" Mencius said, "If he loves and protects the people, it is impossible to prevent him from attaining it."

The king said, "Is such an one as poor I competent to love and protect the people?" "Yes," was the reply. "From what do you know that I am competent to that?" "I have heard," said Mencius, "from Hoo Heih the following incident:—'The king,' said he, 'was sitting aloft in the hall, when some people appeared leading a bull past below it. The king saw it, and asked where the bull was going, and being answered that they were going to consecrate a bell with its blood, he said, "Let it go, I cannot bear its frightened appearance—as if it were an innocent person going to the place of death." They asked in reply whether, if they did so, they should omit the consecration of the bell, but the king said, "How can that be omitted? Change it for a sheep." I do not know whether this incident occurred."

"It did," said the king, and Mencius replied, "The heart seen in this is sufficient to carry you to the Royal sway. The people all supposed that your Majesty grudged the animal, but your servant knows surely that it was your Majesty's not being able to bear the sight of the creature's distress which made you do as you did."

The king said, "You are right; and yet there really was an appearance of what the people imagined. But though Ts'e be narrow and small, how should I grudge a bull? Indeed it was because I could not bear its frightened appearance, as if it were an innocent person going to the place of death, that therefore I changed it for a sheep."

Mencius said, "Let not your Majesty deem it strange that the people should think you grudged the animal. When you changed a large one for a small, how should they know the true reason? If you felt pained by its being led without any guilt to the place of death, what was there to choose between a bull and a sheep?" The king laughed and said, "What really was my mind in the matter? I did not grudge the value of the bull, and yet I changed it for a sheep! There was reason in the people's saying that I grudged the creature."

Mencius said, "There is no harm in their saying so. It was an artifice of benevolence. You saw the bull, and had not seen the sheep. So is the superior man affected towards animals, that, having seen them alive, he cannot bear to see them die, and, having heard their dying cries, he cannot bear to eat their flesh. On this account he keeps away from his stalls and kitchen."

The king was pleased and said, "The Ode says,

'What other men have in their minds,
I can measure by reflection.'

This might be spoken of you, my Master. I indeed did the thing, but when I turned my thoughts inward and sought for it, I could not discover my own mind. When you, Master, spoke those words, the movements of compassion began to work in my mind. But how is it that this heart has in it what is equal to the attainment of the Royal sway?"

Mencius said, "Suppose a man were to make this statement to your Majesty, 'My strength is sufficient to lift three thousand catties, but is not sufficient to lift one feather; my eyesight is sharp enough to examine the point of an autumn hair, but I do not see a wagon-load of fagots,' would your Majesty allow what he said?" "No," was the king's remark, and Mencius proceeded, "Now here is kindness sufficient to reach to animals, and yet no benefits are extended from it to the people—how is this? is an exception to be made here? The truth is, the feather's not being lifted is because the strength was not used; the wagon-load of firewood's not being seen is because the eyesight was not used; and the people's not being loved and protected is because the kindness is not used. Therefore your Majesty's not attaining to the Royal sway is because you do not do it, and not because you are not able to do it."

The king asked, "How may the difference between him who does not do a thing and him who is not able to do it be graphically set forth?" Mencius replied, "In such a thing as taking the T'ae mountain under your arm, and leaping with it over the North Sea, if you say to people, 'I am not able to do it,' that is a real case of not being able. In such a matter as breaking off a branch from a tree at the order of a superior, if you say to people, 'I am not able to do it,' it is not a case of not being able to do it. And so your Majesty's not attaining to the Royal sway is not such a case as that of taking the T'ae mountain under your arm and leaping over the North Sea with it; but it is a case like that of breaking off a branch from a tree.

"Treat with reverence due to age the elders in your own family, so that those in the families of others shall be similarly treated; treat with the kindness due to youth the young in your own family, so that those in the families of others shall be similarly treated—do this and the kingdom may be made to go round in your palm. It is said in the 'Book of Poetry,'

> 'His example acted on his wife,
> Extended to his brethren,
> And was felt by all the clans and States;'

telling us how King Wan simply took this kindly heart, and exercised it towards those parties. Therefore the carrying out of the feeling of kindness by a ruler will suffice for the love and protection of all within the four seas; and if he do not carry it out, he will not be able to protect his wife and children. The way in which the ancients came greatly to surpass other men was no other than this, that they carried out well what they did, so as to affect others. Now your kindness is sufficient to reach to animals, and yet no benefits are extended from it to the people. How is this? Is an exception to be made here?

"By weighing we know what things are light, and what heavy. By measuring we know what things are long, and what short. All things are so dealt with, and the mind requires specially to be so. I beg your Majesty to measure it.

"Your Majesty collects your equipments of war, endangers your soldiers and officers and excites the resentment of the various princes—do these things cause you pleasure in your mind?"

The king said, "No. How should I derive pleasure from these things? My object in them is to seek for what I greatly desire."

Mencius said, "May I hear from you what it is that your Majesty greatly desires?"

The king laughed, and did not speak. Mencius resumed, "Are you led to desire it because you have not enough of rich and sweet food for your mouth? or because you have not enough of light and warm clothing for your body? or because you have not enough of beautifully colored objects to satisfy your eyes? or because there are not voices and sounds enough to fill your ears? or because you have not enough of attendants and favorites to stand before you and receive your orders? Your Majesty's various officers are sufficient to supply you with all these things. How can your Majesty have such a desire on account of them?" "No," said the king, "my desire is not on account of them." Mencius observed, "Then what your Majesty greatly desires can be known. You desire to enlarge your territories, to have Ts'in and Ts'oo coming to your court, to rule the Middle States, and to attract to you the barbarous tribes that surround them. But to do what you do in order to seek for what you desire is like climbing a tree to seek for fish."

"Is it so bad as that?" said the king. "I apprehend it is worse," was the reply. "If you climb a tree to seek for fish, although you do not get the fish, you have no subsequent calamity. But if you do what you do in order to seek for what you desire, doing it even with all your heart, you will assuredly afterwards meet with calamities." The king said, "May I hear what they will be?" Mencius replied, "If the people of Tsow were fighting with the people of Ts'oo, which of them does your Majesty think would conquer?" "The people of Ts'oo would conquer," was the answer, and Mencius pursued, "So then, a small State cannot contend with a great, few cannot contend with many, nor can the weak contend with the strong. The territory within the seas would embrace nine divisions, each of a thousand li square. All Ts'e together is one of them. If with one part you try to subdue the other eight, what is the difference between that and Tsow's contending with Ts'oo? With the desire which you have, you must turn back to the proper course for its attainment.

"Now, if your Majesty will institute a government whose action shall all be benevolent, this will cause all the officers in the kingdom to wish to stand in your Majesty's court, the farmers all to wish to plough in your Majesty's fields, the merchants, both travelling and stationary, all to wish to store their goods in your Majesty's market-places, travellers and visitors all to wish to travel on your Majesty's roads, and all under heaven who feel aggrieved by their rulers to wish to come and complain to your Majesty. When they are so bent, who will be able to keep them back?"

The king said, "I am stupid and cannot advance to this. But I wish you, my Master, to assist my intentions. Teach me clearly, and although I am deficient in intelligence and vigor, I should like to try at least to institute such a government."

Mencius replied, "They are only men of education, who, without a certain livelihood, are able to maintain a fixed heart. As to the people, if they have not a certain livelihood, they will be found not to have a fixed heart. And if they have not a fixed heart, there is nothing which they will not do in the way of self-abandonment, of moral deflection, of depravity, and of wild license. When they have thus been involved in crime, to follow them up and punish them, is to entrap the people. How can such a thing as entrapping the people be done under the rule of a benevolent man?"

"Therefore, an intelligent ruler will regulate the livelihood of the people, so as to make sure that, above, they shall have sufficient wherewith to serve their parents, and below, sufficient wherewith to support their wives and children; that in good years they shall always be abundantly satisfied, and that in bad years they shall not be in danger of perishing. After this he may urge them, and they will proceed to what is good, for in this case the people will follow after that with readiness.

"But now the livelihood of the people is so regulated, that, above, they have not sufficient wherewith to serve their parents, and, below, they have not sufficient wherewith to support their wives and children; even in good years their lives are always embittered, and in bad years they are in danger of perishing. In such circumstances their only object is to escape from death, and they are afraid they will not succeed in doing so—what leisure have they to cultivate propriety and righteousness?

"If your Majesty wishes to carry out a benevolent government, why not turn back to what is the essential step to its attainment?

"Let mulberry trees be planted about the homesteads with their five acres, and persons of fifty years will be able to wear silk. In keeping fowls, pigs, dogs, and swine, let not their times of breeding be neglected, and persons of seventy years will be able to eat flesh. Let there not be taken away the time that is proper for the cultivation of the field-allotment of a hundred acres, and the family of eight mouths will not suffer from hunger. Let careful attention be paid to the teaching in the various schools, with repeated inculcation of the filial and fraternal duties, and gray-haired men will not be seen upon the roads, carrying burdens on their backs or on their heads. It has never been that the ruler of a State, where these results were seen, the old wearing silk and eating flesh, and the black-haired people suffering neither from hunger nor cold, did not attain to the Royal dignity."

[*Books II, III, and IV are omitted*]

BOOK V

Wan Chang[1]

WAN CHANG asked Mencius, saying, "When Shun went into the fields, he cried out and wept towards the pitying heavens. Why did he cry out and weep?" Mencius replied, "He was dissatisfied and full of earnest desire."

Wan Chang said, "When his parents love him, a son rejoices and forgets them not; and when they hate him, though they punish him, he does not allow himself to be dissatisfied. Was Shun then dissatisfied with his parents?" Mencius said, "Ch'ang Seih asked Kung-ming Kaou, saying, 'As to Shun's going into the fields, I have received your instructions; but I do not understand about his weeping and crying out to the pitying heavens, and to his parents.' Kung-ming Kaou answered him, 'You do not understand that matter.' Now Kung-ming Kaou thought that the heart of a filial son like Shun could not be so free from sorrow as Seih seemed to imagine he might have been. Shun would be saying, 'I exert my strength to cultivate the fields, but I am thereby only discharging my duty as a son. What is there wrong in me that my parents do not love me?'

"The emperor caused his own children—nine sons and two daughters—the various officers, oxen and sheep, store-

---

[1] The Book is named from Wan Chang, who is almost the only interlocutor with Mencius in it. The tradition is that it was in company with Wan's disciples that Mencius, baffled in all his hopes of doing public service, and having retired into privacy, composed the Seven Books which constitute his works. The part which follows is all occupied with discussions in vindication of Shun and other ancient worthies.

houses and granaries, all to be prepared for the service of
Shun amid the channeled fields. Most of the officers in the
empire repaired to him. The emperor designed that he
should superintend the empire along with himself, and
then to transfer it to him. But because his parents were not
in accord with him, he felt like a poor man who has nowhere to turn to.

"To be an object of complacency to the officers of the
empire is what men desire; but it was not sufficient to remove the sorrow of Shun. The possession of beauty is what
men desire: but though Shun had for his wives the two
daughters of the emperor, it was not sufficient to remove
his sorrow. Riches are what men desire, but though the
empire was the rich property of Shun, it was not enough
to remove his sorrow. Honors are what men desire, but
though Shun had the dignity of being the son of Heaven,
it was not sufficient to remove his sorrow. The reason why
his being the object of men's complacency, the possession
of beauty, riches, and honors, could not remove his sorrow
was because it could be removed only by his being in en-
tire accord with his parents.

"The desire of a child is towards his father and mother.
When he becomes conscious of the attractions of beauty,
his desire is towards young and beautiful women. When he
comes to have a wife and children, his desire is towards
them. When he obtains office, his desire is towards his
ruler; and if he cannot get the regard of his ruler, he burns
within. But the man of great filial piety, all his life, has his
desire towards his parents. In the great Shun I see the case
of one whose desire was towards them when he was fifty
years old."

Wan Chang asked Mencius, saying, "It is said in the
'Book of Poetry,'

> 'How do we proceed in taking a wife?
> Announcement must first be made to our parents.'

If the rule be indeed as thus expressed, no one ought to have illustrated it so well as Shun—how was it that Shun's marriage took place without his informing his parents?" Mencius replied, "If he had informed them, he would not have been able to marry. That male and female dwell together is the greatest of human relations. If Shun had informed his parents, he must have made void this greatest of human relations, and incurred thereby their resentment. It was on this account that he did not inform them."

Wan Chang said, "As to Shun's marrying without making announcement to his parents, I have heard your instructions. But how was it that the emperor gave him his daughters as wives without informing his parents?" Mencius said, "The emperor also knew that, if he informed his parents, he could not have given him his daughters as wives."

Wan Chang said, "His parents set Shun to repair a granary, and then removed the ladder by which he had ascended; after which Koo-sow set fire to it. They sent him to dig a well, from which he managed to get out; but they, not knowing this, proceeded to cover it up. His brother, Sëang, said, 'Of this scheme to cover up the city-farming gentleman the merit is all mine. Let my parents have his oxen and sheep; let them have his granaries and storehouses. His shield and spear shall be mine; his lute shall be mine; his carved bow shall be mine; and I will make his two wives attend for me to my bed.' Sëang then went away and entered Shun's house, and there was Shun upon a couch with his lute. Sëang said, 'I am come simply because I was thinking anxiously about you,' and at the same time he looked ashamed. Shun said to him, 'There are all my officers; do you take the management of them for me.' I do not know whether Shun was ignorant of Sëang's wishing to kill him." Mencius replied, "How could he be ignorant of it? But when Sëang was sorrowful, he was also sorrowful, and when Sëang was joyful, he was also joyful."

Wan Chang continued, "Then was Shun one who re-joiced hypocritically?" "No," was the reply. "Formerly some one sent a present of a live fish to Tsze-ch'an of Ch'ing. Tsze-ch'an ordered his pond-keeper to feed it in the pond; but the man cooked it and reported the execu-tion of his commission, saying, 'When I first let it go, it looked embarrassed. In a little while it seemed to be some-what at ease, and then it swam away as if delighted.' 'It had got into its element!' said Tsze-ch'an. The pond-keeper went out and said, 'Who calls Tsze-ch'an wise? When I had cooked and eaten the fish, he said, "It has got into its element! It has got into its element!"' Thus a superior man may be imposed on by what seems to be as it ought to be, but it is difficult to entrap him by what is contrary to right principle. Sëang came in the way in which the love of his elder brother would have made him come, and therefore Shun truly believed him, and rejoiced at it. What hypoc-risy was there?"

Wan Chang said, "Sëang made it his daily business to kill Shun; why was it that, when the latter was raised to be the son of Heaven, he only banished him?" Mencius re-plied, "He invested him with a State, and some have said that it was banishing him." When Chang said, "Shun ban-ished the Superintendent of Works to Yëw-chow, sent away Hwan-tow to Mount Ts'ung, slew the Prince of San Mëaou in San-wei, and imprisoned K'wan on Mount Yu. When those four criminals were thus dealt with, all under heaven submitted to him; it was a cutting off of men who were destitute of benevolence. But Sëang was of all men the most destitute of benevolence, and Shun invested him with the State of Pe; of what crime had the people of Pe been guilty? Does a benevolent man really act thus? In the case of other men, he cut them off; in the case of his brother, he invested him with a State." Mencius replied,

"A benevolent man does not lay up anger, nor cherish resentment against his brother, but only regards him with affection and love. Regarding him with affection, he wishes him to enjoy honor; loving him, he wishes him to be rich. The investing him with Pe was to enrich and ennoble him. If while Shun himself was emperor, his brother had been a common man, could he have been said to regard him with affection and love?"

Wan Chang said, "I venture to ask what is meant by some saying that it was a banishing of Sëang." Mencius replied, "Sëang could do nothing of himself in his State. The emperor appointed an officer to manage its government, and to pay over its revenues to him; and therefore it was said that it was a banishing of him? How indeed could he be allowed the means of oppressing the people there? Nevertheless, Shun wished to be continually seeing him, and therefore he came unceasingly to court, as is signified in that expression, 'He did not wait for the rendering of tribute, or affairs of government, to receive the prince of Pe.'"

Hëen-k'ëw Mung asked Mencius, saying, "There is the old saying, 'An officer of complete virtue cannot be employed as a minister by his ruler, nor treated as a son by his father.' Shun stood with his face to the south, and Yaou, at the head of all the feudal princes, appeared in his court with his face to the north. Koo-sow also appeared at Shun's court with his face to the north; and when Shun saw him, his countenance assumed a look of distress. Confucius said, 'At this time the empire was in a perilous condition indeed! How unsettled was its state!' I do not know whether what is thus said really took place." Mencius said, "No. These are not the words of a superior man, but the sayings of an uncultivated person of the east of Ts'e. When Yaou was old, Shun took the management of affairs for him. It is said in the Canon of Yaou, 'After twenty-eight years, Fang-

heun demised, and the people mourned for him as for a
parent three years. All within the four seas, the eight instruments of music were stopped and hushed." Confucius
said, 'There are not two suns in the sky, nor two sovereigns
over the people. If Shun had already been in the position
of the son of Heaven, and had moreover led on all the
feudal princes of the empire to observe the three years'
mourning for Yaou, there must in that case have been two
sons of Heaven.'"

Hëen-k'ëw Mung said, "On the point of Shun's not employing Yaou as a minister, I have received your instructions. But it is said in the 'Book of Poetry,'

> 'Under the wide heaven,
> All is the king's land;
> Within the sea-boundaries of the land,
> All are the king's servants.'

When Shun became emperor, I venture to ask how it was
that Koo-sow was not one of his servants." Mencius replied, "That Ode is not to be understood in that way; it
speaks of being laboriously engaged in the king's business,
and not being able to nourish one's parents, as if the subject of it said, 'This is all the king's business, but I alone am
supposed to have ability, and made to toil in it.' Therefore
those who explain the Odes must not insist on one term so
as to do violence to a sentence, nor on a sentence so as to
do violence to the general scope. They must try with their
thoughts to meet that scope, and then they will apprehend
it. If we simply take single sentences, there is that in the
Ode called the 'Yun Han,'

> 'Of the remnant of Chow, among the black-haired people,
> There will not be half a man left.'

If it had really been as thus expressed, then not an individual of the people of Chow would have been left.

"Of all that a filial son can attain to, there is nothing

greater than his honoring his parents. Of what can be attained to in honoring one's parents, there is nothing greater than the nourishing them with the empire. To be the father of the son of Heaven is the height of honor. To be nourished with the empire is the height of nourishment. In this was verified the sentiment in the 'Book of Poetry,'

> 'Ever thinking how to be filial,
> His filial mind was the model which he supplied.'

"In the 'Book of History' it is said, 'With respectful service he appeared before Koo-sow, looking grave and awe-struck, till Koo-sow also was transformed by his example.' This is the true case of the scholar of complete virtue not being treated as a son by his father."

Wan Chang said, "It is said that Yaou gave the empire to Shun; was it so?" Mencius replied, "No; the emperor cannot give the empire to another." "Yes; but Shun possessed the empire. Who gave it to him?" "Heaven gave it to him," was the reply.

"'Heaven gave it to him'; did Heaven confer the appointment on him with specific injunctions?" Mencius said, "No; Heaven does not speak. It simply showed its will by his personal conduct, and by his conduct of affairs."

"'It showed its will by his personal conduct, and by his conduct of affairs,'" returned the other; "how was this?" Mencius said, "The emperor can present a man to Heaven, but he cannot make Heaven give that man the empire. A feudal prince can present a man to the emperor to take his place, but he cannot make the emperor give the princedom to that man. A great officer can present a man to his prince, but he cannot cause the prince to make that man a great officer in his own room. Anciently Yaou presented Shun to Heaven, and Heaven accepted him; he displayed him to the people, and the people accepted him. Therefore I say, 'Heaven does not speak. It simply indicated its will by his personal conduct, and by his conduct of affairs.'"

Chang said, "I presume to ask how it was that Yaou presented Shun to Heaven, and Heaven accepted him, and displayed him to the people, and the people accepted him." The reply was, "He caused him to preside over the sacrifices, and all the Spirits were well pleased with them; thus it was that Heaven accepted him. He caused him to preside over the conduct of affairs, and affairs were well administered, so that all the people reposed under him; thus it was that the people accepted him. Heaven gave the empire to him, and the people gave it to him. Therefore I said, 'The emperor cannot give the empire to another.'

"Shun assisted Yaou in the government for twenty and eight years; this was more than man could have done, and was from Heaven. When the three years' mourning consequent on the death of Yaou were accomplished, Shun withdrew from the son of Yaou to the south of the southern Ho. The princes of the empire, however, repairing to court, went not to the son of Yaou, but to Shun. Litigants went not to the son of Yaou, but to Shun. Singers sang not the son of Yaou, but Shun. Therefore I said that it was Heaven that gave him the empire. It was after this that he went to the Middle State, and occupied the seat of the son of Heaven. If he had before these things taken up his residence in the palace of Yaou, and applied pressure to his son, it would have been an act of usurpation, and not the gift of Heaven.

"This view of Shun's obtaining the empire is in accordance with what is said in The Great Declaration—'Heaven sees as my people see, Heaven hears as my people hear.'"

Wan Chang said, "People say, 'When the disposal of the empire came to Yu, his virtue was inferior to that of Yaou and Shun, and he did not transmit it to the worthiest, but to his son.' Was it so?" Mencius replied, "No; it was not so. When Heaven gave the empire to the worthiest, it was given to the worthiest; when Heaven gave it to the son of the preceding emperor, it was given to that son. Formerly Shun presented Yu to Heaven for a period of seventeen years; and when the three years' mourning, consequent on the death of Shun, were accomplished, Yu withdrew from the son of Yu to Yang-shing. The people of the empire followed him as, after the death of Yaou, they had not followed his son, but followed Shun. Yu presented Yih to Heaven for a period of seven years; and when the three years' mourning consequent on the death of Yu were accomplished, Yih withdrew from the son of Yu to the north of Mount Ke. The princes repairing to court, and litigants, went not to Yih, but to K'e, saying, 'He is the son of our ruler.' Singers did not sing Yih, but they sang K'e, saying, 'He is the son of our ruler.'

"That Tan-choo was not equal to his father, and Shun's son also not equal to his; that Shun assisted Yaou, and Yu assisted Shun, for a period of many years, conferring benefits on the people for a long time; that K'e was virtuous and able, and could reverently enter into and continue the ways of Yu; that Yih assisted Yu for a period of a few years, conferring benefits on the people not for a long time; that the length of time that Shun, Yu, and Yih, assisted in the government was so different; and that the sons of the emperors were one a man of talents and virtue, and the other two inferior to their fathers:—all these things were from Heaven, and what could not be produced by man. That which is done without any one's seeming to do it is from Heaven. That which comes to pass without any one's seeming to bring it about is from Heaven.

"In the case of a private man's obtaining the empire, there must be in him virtue equal to that of Shun and Yu, and moreover there must be the presenting him to Heaven by the preceding emperor. It was on this latter account that Chung-ne did not obtain the kingdom.

"When the throne descends by natural succession, he

who is displaced by Heaven must be like Këeh or Chow. It was on this account that Yih, E Yin, and the duke of Chow did not obtain the kingdom.

"E Yin assisted T'ang so that he became sovereign of the kingdom. After the demise of T'ang, T'ae-ting having died without being appointed in his place, Wae-ping reigned two years, and Chung-jin four. T'ae-Këah then was turning upside down the canons and examples of T'ang, and E Yin placed him in T'ung for three years. There he repented of his errors, was contrite, and reformed himself. In T'ung he came to dwell in benevolence and moved towards righteousness, during those three years listening to the lessons given to him by E Yin, after which that minister again returned with him to Poh.

"The duke of Chow's not getting the kingdom was like that of Yih's not getting the throne of Hëa, or E Yin's that of Yin.

"Confucius said, 'T'ang and Yu resigned the throne to the worthiest; the founders of the Hëa, Yin, and Chow dynasties transmitted it to their sons. The principle of righteousness was the same in all the cases.'"

Wan Chang asked Mencius, saying, "People say that E Yin sought an introduction to T'ang by his knowledge of cookery; was it so?" Mencius replied, "No, it was not so. E Yin was farming in the lands of the State of Sin, delighting in the principles of Yaou and Shun. In any matter contrary to the righteousness which they prescribed, or to the course which they enjoined, though he had been salaried with the empire, he would not have regarded it; though there had been yoked for him a thousand teams, he would not have looked at them. In any matter contrary to the righteousness which they prescribed, or to the course which they enjoined, he would not have given nor taken even a single straw.

"T'ang sent persons with presents of silk to ask him to

enter his service. With an air of indifference and self-satisfaction, he said, 'What can I do with these silks with which T'ang invites me? Is it not best for me to abide in these channeled fields, and therein delight myself with the principles of Yaou and Shun?'

"T'ang thrice sent persons thus to invite him. After this, with the change of purpose displayed in his countenance, he spoke in a different style, saying, 'Instead of abiding in the channeled fields, and therein delighting myself with the principles of Yaou and Shun, had I not better make this ruler one after the style of Yaou and Shun? had I not better make this people like the people of Yaou and Shun? had I not better in my own person see these things for myself? Heaven's plan in the production of this people is this:—That they who are first informed, should instruct those who are later in being informed, and those who first apprehend principles should instruct those who are slower to do so. I am the one of Heaven's people who have first apprehended; I will take these principles and instruct this people in them. If I do not instruct them, who will do so?'

"He thought that among all the people of the kingdom, even the private men and women, if there were any that did not enjoy such benefits as Yaou and Shun conferred, it was as if he himself pushed them into a ditch. He took upon himself the heavy charge of all under Heaven in this way, and therefore he went to T'ang, and pressed upon him the duty of attacking Hëa, and saving the people.

"I have not heard of one who bent himself and at the same time made others straight; how much less could one disgrace himself, and thereby rectify the whole kingdom? The actions of the sages have been different. Some have kept far away from office, and others have drawn near to it; some have left their offices, and others have not done so; that in which these different courses all meet, is simply the keeping of their persons pure.

"I have heard that E Yin sought an introduction to T'ang by the principles of Yaou and Shun; I have not heard he did so by his knowledge of cookery.

"In the 'Instructions of E,' it is said, 'Heaven, destroying Këeh, commenced attacking him in the palace of Muh; we commenced in Poh.'"

Wan Chang asked Mencius, saying, "Some say that Confucius in Wei lived with an ulcer-doctor, and in Ts'e with Tseih Hwan, the chief of the eunuchs; was it so?" Mencius said, "No, it was not so. Those are the inventions of men fond of strange things.

"In Wei he lived in the house of Yen Ch'ow-yëw. The wife of the officer Mei and the wife of Tsze-lu were sisters. Mei-tsze spoke to Tsze-lu, saying, 'If Confucius will lodge with me, he may get to be a high noble of Wei.' Tsze-lu reported this to Confucius, who said, 'That is as ordered by Heaven.' Confucius advanced according to propriety, and retired according to righteousness. In regard to his obtaining office and honor or not obtaining them, he said, 'That is as ordered.' But if he had lodged with an ulcer-doctor and with Tseih Hwan, the chief of the eunuchs, that would neither have been according to righteousness nor any ordering of Heaven.

"When Confucius, being dissatisfied in Lu and Wei, had left those States, he met with the attempt of Hwan, the master of the Horse, in Sung, to intercept and kill him, so that he had to pass through Sung in the dress of a private man. At that time, though he was in circumstances of distress, he lodged in the house of Ching-tsze, the minister of works, who was then a minister of Chow, the marquis of Ch'in.

"I have heard that ministers in the service of a court may be known from those to whom they are hosts, and that ministers coming from a distance may be known from those with whom they lodge. If Confucius had lodged with an ulcer-doctor and with Tseih Hwan, the chief of the eunuchs, how could he have been Confucius?"

Wan Chang asked Mencius, saying, "Some say that Pih-le He sold himself to a cattle-keeper of Ts'in for five sheep-skins, and fed his cattle for him, to seek an introduction to Duke Muh of Ts'in; is this true?" Mencius said, "No, it was not so. This is the invention of some one fond of strange things.

"Pih-le He was a man of Yu. The people of Ts'in by the inducement of a *peih* of Ch'uy-Keih and a team of Këuh-ch'an horses were asking liberty to march through Yu to attack Kwoh. Kung Che-k'e remonstrated with the duke of Yu, asking him not to grant their request, but Pih-le He did not remonstrate.

"When he knew that the duke of Yu was not to be remonstrated with, and went in consequence from that State to Ts'in, he had reached the age of seventy. If by that time he did not know that it would be a disgraceful thing to seek for an introduction to Duke Muh of Ts'in by feeding cattle, could he be called wise? But not remonstrating where it was of no use to remonstrate, could he be said not to be wise? Knowing that the duke of Yu would be ruined, and leaving his State before that event, he could not be said to be not wise. As soon as he was advanced in Ts'in, he knew that Duke Muh was one with whom he could have a field for action, and became chief minister to him; could he be said to be not wise? Acting as chief minister in Ts'in, he made his ruler distinguished throughout the kingdom, and worthy to be handed down to future ages; if he had not been a man of talents and virtue, could he have done this? As to selling himself in order to bring about the destruction of his ruler, even a villager who had a regard for himself, would not do such a thing; and shall we say that a man of talents and virtue did it?"

THE SHI-KING

[Metrical translation by James Legge]

INTRODUCTION

The wisdom of Confucius as a social reformer, as a teacher and guide of the Chinese people, is shown in many ways. He not only gave them a code of personal deportment, providing them with rules for the etiquette and ceremony of life, but he instilled into them that profound spirit of domestic piety which is one of the strongest features in the Chinese character. He took measures to secure also the intellectual cultivation of his followers, and his Five Canons contain all the most ancient works of Chinese literature, in the departments of poetry, history, philosophy, and legislation. The Shi-King is a collection of Chinese poetry made by Confucius himself. This great anthology consists of more than three hundred pieces, covering the whole range of Chinese lyric poetry, the oldest of which dates some eighteen centuries before Christ, while the latest of the selections must have been written at the beginning of the sixth century before Christ. These poems are of the highest interest, and even nowadays may be read with delight by Europeans. The ballad and the hymn are among the earliest forms of national poetry, and the contents of the Shi-King naturally show specimens of lyric poetry of this sort. We find there not only hymns, but also ballads of a really fine and spirited character. Sometimes the poems celebrate the common pursuits, occupations, and incidents of life. They rise to the exaltation of the epithalamium, or of the vintage song; at other times they deal with sentiment and human conduct, being in the highest degree sententious and epigrammatic. We must give the credit to

Confucius of having saved for us the literature of China, and of having set his people an example in preserving the monuments of a remote antiquity. While the literatures of ancient Greece and Rome have largely perished in the convulsions that followed the breaking up of the Roman empire in Europe, when the kingdom of China fell into disorder and decrepitude this one great teacher stepped forward to save the precious record of historic fact, philosophical thought, and of legislation as well as poetry, from being swept away by the deluge of revolution. Confucius showed his wisdom by the high value he set upon the poetry of his native land, and his name must be set side by side with that of the astute tyrant of Athens who collected the poems of Homer and preserved them as a precious heritage to the Greek world. Confucius has given us his opinion with regard to the poems of the Shi-King. No man, he says, is worth speaking to who has not mastered the poems of an anthology, the perusal of which elevates the mind and purifies it from all corrupt thoughts. Thanks to the work of modern scholarship, English readers can now verify this dictum for themselves.

E. W.

BOOK I

The Odes of Chow and the South

CELEBRATING THE VIRTUE OF KING WAN'S BRIDE

Hark! from the islet in the stream the voice
Of the fish-hawks that o'er their nests rejoice!
From them our thoughts to that young lady go,
Modest and virtuous, loth herself to show.
Where could be found to share our prince's state,
So fair, so virtuous, and so fit a mate?

See how the duckweed's stalks, or short or long,
Sway left and right, as moves the current strong!
So hard it was for him the maid to find!
By day, by night, our prince with constant mind
Sought for her long, but all his search was vain.
Awake, asleep, he ever felt the pain
Of longing thought, as when on restless bed,
Tossing about, one turns his fevered head.

Here long, there short, afloat the duckweed lies;
But caught at last, we seize the longed-for prize.
The maiden modest, virtuous, coy, is found;
Strike every lute, and joyous welcome sound.
Ours now, the duckweed from the stream we bear,
And cook to use with other viands rare.
He has the maiden, modest, virtuous, bright;
Let bells and drums proclaim our great delight.

CELEBRATING THE INDUSTRY OF KING WAN'S QUEEN

Sweet was the scene. The spreading dolichos
Extended far, down to the valley's depths,
With leaves luxuriant. The orioles
Fluttered around, and on the bushy trees
In throngs collected—whence their pleasant notes
Resounded far in richest melody.

The spreading dolichos extended far,
Covering the valley's sides, down to its depths,
With leaves luxuriant and dense. I cut
It down, then boiled, and from the fibres spun
Of cloth, both fine and coarse, large store,
To wear, unwearied of such simple dress.

Now back to my old home, my parents dear
To see, I go. The matron I have told,
Who will announcement make. Meanwhile my clothes,
My private clothes I wash, and rinse my robes.
Which of them need be rinsed? and which need not?
My parents dear to visit, back I go.

IN PRAISE OF A BRIDE

Graceful and young the peach-tree stands;
   How rich its flowers, all gleaming bright!
This bride to her new home repairs;
   Chamber and house she'll order right.

Graceful and young the peach-tree stands;
   Large crops of fruit it soon will show.
This bride to her new home repairs;
   Chamber and house her sway shall know.

Graceful and young the peach-tree stands,
Its foliage clustering green and full.
This bride to her new home repairs;
Her household will attest her rule.

CELEBRATING T'AE-SZE'S FREEDOM FROM JEALOUSY

In the South are the trees whose branches are bent,
And droop in such fashion that o'er their extent
All the dolichos' creepers fast cling.
See our princely lady, from whom we have got
Rejoicing that's endless! May her happy lot
And her honors repose ever bring!

In the South are the trees whose branches are bent,
And droop in such fashion that o'er their extent
All the dolichos' creepers are spread.
See our princely lady, from whom we have got
Rejoicing that's endless! Of her happy lot
And her honors the greatness ne'er fade!

In the South are the trees whose branches are bent,
And droop in such fashion that o'er their extent
All the dolichos' creepers entwine.
See our princely lady, from whom we have got
Rejoicing that's endless! May her happy lot
And her honors complete ever shine!

THE FRUITFULNESS OF THE LOCUST

Ye locusts, wingèd tribes,
Gather in concord fine;
Well your descendants may
In numerous bright hosts shine!

Ye locusts, wingèd tribes,
   Your wings in flight resound;
Well your descendants may
   In endless lines be found!

Ye locusts, wingèd tribes,
   Together cluster strong;
Well your descendants may
   In swarms forever throng!

LAMENTING THE ABSENCE OF A CHERISHED FRIEND

Though small my basket, all my toil
   Filled it with mouse-ears but in part.
I set it on the path, and sighed
   For the dear master of my heart.

My steeds, o'er-tasked, their progress stayed,
   When midway up that rocky height.
Give me a cup from that gilt vase—
   When shall this longing end in sight?

To mount that lofty ridge I drove,
   Until my steeds all changed their hue.
A cup from that rhinoceros's horn
   May help my longing to subdue.

Striving to reach that flat-topped hill,
   My steeds, worn out, relaxed their strain;
My driver also sank oppressed:—
   I'll never see my lord again!

CELEBRATING THE GOODNESS OF THE DESCENDANTS OF KING WAN

As the feet of the *lin,* which avoid each living thing,
So our prince's noble sons no harm to men will bring.
They are the *lin!*

As the front of the *lin,* never forward thrust in wrath,
So our prince's noble grandsons of love tread the path.
They are the *lin!*

As the horn of the *lin,* flesh-tipped, no wound to give,
So our prince's noble kindred kindly with all live.
They are the *lin!*

[NOTE.—The "lin" is the female of "K'e"—a fabulous animal—the symbol of all goodness and benevolence; having the body of a deer, the tail of an ox, the hoofs of a horse, one horn, the scales of a fish, etc. Its feet do not tread on any living thing—not even on live grass; it does not butt with its forehead; and the end of its horn is covered with flesh—to show that, while able for war, it wills to have peace. The "lin" was supposed to appear inaugurating a golden age, but the poet finds a better auspice of that in the character of Wan's family and kindred.]

THE VIRTUOUS MANNERS OF THE YOUNG WOMEN

High and compressed, the Southern trees
No shelter from the sun afford.
The girls free ramble by the Han,
But will not hear enticing word.
Like the broad Han are they,
Through which one cannot dive;
And like the Keang's long stream,
Wherewith no raft can strive.

Many the fagots bound and piled;
  The thorns I'd hew still more to make.
As brides, those girls their new homes seek;
  Their colts to feed I'd undertake.
Like the broad Han are they,
  Through which one cannot dive;
And like the Keang's long stream,
  Wherewith no raft can strive.

Many the fagots bound and piled;
  The Southern-wood I'd cut for more.
As brides, those girls their new homes seek;
  Food for their colts I'd bring large store.
Like the broad Han are they,
  Through which one cannot dive;
And like the Keang's long stream,
  Wherewith no raft can strive.

PRAISE OF A RABBIT-CATCHER

Careful he sets his rabbit-nets all round;
Chang-chang his blows upon the pegs resound.
Stalwart the man and bold! his bearing all
Shows he might be his prince's shield and wall.

Careful he is his rabbit-nets to place
Where many paths of rabbits' feet bear trace.
Stalwart the man and bold! 'tis plain to see
He to his prince companion good would be.

Careful he is his rabbit-nets to spread,
Where in the forest's depth the trees give shade.
Stalwart the man and bold! fit his the part
Guide to his prince to be, and faithful heart.

THE SONG OF THE PLANTAIN-GATHERERS

We gather and gather the plantains;
　Come gather them anyhow.
Yes, gather and gather the plantains,
　And here we have got them now.

We gather and gather the plantains;
　Now off the ears we must tear.
Yes, gather and gather the plantains,
　And now the seeds are laid bare.

We gather and gather the plantains,
　The seeds in our skirts are placed.
Yes, gather and gather the plantains.
　Ho! safe in the girdled waist!

THE AFFECTION OF THE WIVES ON THE JOO

Along the raised banks of the Joo,
　To hew slim stem and branch I wrought,
My lord away, my husband true,
　Like hunger-pang my troubled thought!

Along the raised banks of the Joo,
　Branch and fresh shoot confessed my art.
I've seen my lord, my husband true,
　And still he folds me in his heart.

As the toiled bream makes red its tail,
　Toil you, Sir, for the Royal House;
Amidst its blazing fires, nor quail:—
　Your parents see you pay your vows.

BOOK II

The Odes of Shaou and the South

THE MARRIAGE OF A PRINCESS

In the magpie's nest
Dwells the dove at rest.
This young bride goes to her future home;
To meet her a hundred chariots come.

Of the magpie's nest
Is the dove possessed.
This bride goes to her new home to live;
And escort a hundred chariots give.

The nest magpie wove
Now filled by the dove.
This bride now takes to her home her way;
And these numerous cars her state display.

THE INDUSTRY AND REVERENCE OF A PRINCE'S WIFE

Around the pools, the islets o'er,
    Fast she plucks white Southern-wood,
To help the sacrificial store;
    And for our prince does service good.

152

Where streams among the valleys shine,
  Of Southern-woods she plucks the white;
And brings it to the sacred shrine,
  To aid our prince in solemn rite.

In head-dress high, most reverent, she
  The temple seeks at early dawn.
The service o'er, the head-dress see
  To her own chamber slow withdrawn.

THE WIFE OF SOME GREAT OFFICER BEWAILS HIS ABSENCE

Shrill chirp the insects in the grass;
  All about the hoppers spring.
While I my husband do not see,
  Sorrow must my bosom wring.
    O to meet him!
    O to greet him!
  Then my heart would rest and sing.

Ascending high that Southern hill,
  Turtle ferns I strove to get.
While I my husband do not see,
  Sorrow must my heart beset.
    O to meet him!
    O to greet him!
  Then my heart would cease to fret.

Ascending high that Southern hill,
  Spinous ferns I sought to find.
While I my husband do not see,
  Rankles sorrow in my mind.
    O to meet him!
    O to greet him!
  In my heart would peace be shrined.

THE DILIGENCE OF THE YOUNG WIFE OF AN OFFICER

She gathers fast the large duckweed,
   From valley stream that southward flows;
And for the pondweed to the pools
   Left on the plains by floods she goes.

The plants, when closed her toil, she puts
   In baskets round and baskets square.
Then home she hies to cook her spoil,
   In pans and tripods ready there.

In sacred chamber this she sets,
   Where the light falls down through the wall.
'Tis she, our lord's young reverent wife,
   Who manages this service all.

THE LOVE OF THE PEOPLE FOR THE DUKE OF SHAOU

O fell not that sweet pear-tree!
  See how its branches spread.
    Spoil not its shade,
    For Shaou's chief laid
  Beneath it his weary head.

O clip not that sweet pear-tree!
  Each twig and leaflet spare.
    'Tis sacred now,
    Since the lord of Shaou,
  When weary, rested him there.

O touch not that sweet pear-tree!
Bend not a twig of it now.
There long ago,
As the stories show,
Oft halted the chief of Shaou.

THE EASY DIGNITY OF THE OFFICERS AT SOME COURT

Arrayed in skins of lamb or sheep,
 With five silk braidings all of white,
From court they go, to take their meal,
 All self-possessed, with spirits light.

How on their skins of lamb or sheep
 The five seams wrought with white silk show!
With easy steps, and self-possessed,
 From court to take their meal, they go.

Upon their skins of lamb or sheep
 Shines the white silk the seams to link.
With easy steps and self-possessed,
 They go from court to eat and drink.

ANXIETY OF A YOUNG LADY TO GET MARRIED

Ripe, the plums fall from the bough;
Only seven-tenths left there now!
Ye whose hearts on me are set,
Now the time is fortunate!

Ripe, the plums fall from the bough;
Only three-tenths left there now!
Ye who wish my love to gain,
Will not now apply in vain!

No more plums upon the bough!
All are in my basket now!
Ye who me with ardor seek,
Need the word but freely speak!

BOOK III

The Odes of P'ei

AN OFFICER BEWAILS THE NEGLECT WITH WHICH HE IS
TREATED

It floats about, that boat of cypress wood,
   Now here, now there, as by the current borne.
Nor rest nor sleep comes in my troubled mood;
   I suffer as when painful wound has torn
   The shrinking body. Thus I dwell forlorn,
And aimless muse, my thoughts of sorrow full.
   I might with wine refresh my spirit worn;
I might go forth, and, sauntering try to cool
The fever of my heart; but grief holds sullen rule.

My mind resembles not a mirror plate,
   Reflecting all the impressions it receives.
The good I love, the bad regard with hate;
   I only cherish whom my heart believes.
   Colleagues I have, but yet my spirit grieves,
That on their honor I cannot depend.
   I speak, but my complaint no influence leaves
Upon their hearts; with mine no feelings blend;
With me in anger they, and fierce disdain contend.

My mind is fixed, and cannot, like a stone,
   Be turned at will indifferently about;
And what I think, to that, and that alone,

I utterance give, alike within, without;
   Nor can like mat be rolled and carried out.
With dignity in presence of them all,
   My conduct marked, my goodness who shall scout?
My foes I boldly challenge, great and small,
If there be aught in me they can in question call.

How full of trouble is my anxious heart!
   With hate the blatant herd of creatures mean
Ceaseless pursue. Of their attacks the smart
   Keeps my mind in distress. Their venomed spleen
   Aye vents itself; and with insulting mien
They vex my soul; and no one on my side
   A word will speak. Silent, alone, unseen,
I think of my sad case; then opening wide
My eyes, as if from sleep, I beat my breast, sore-tried.

Thy disc, O sun, should ever be complete,
   While thine, O changing moon, doth wax and wane.
But now our sun hath waned, weak and effete,
   And moons are ever full. My heart with pain
   Is firmly bound, and held in sorrow's chain,
As to the body cleaves an unwashed dress.
   Silent I think of my sad case; in vain
I try to find relief from my distress.
Would I had wings to fly where ills no longer press!

A WIFE DEPLORES THE ABSENCE OF HER HUSBAND

Away the startled pheasant flies,
   With lazy movement of his wings.
Borne was my heart's lord from my eyes;—
   What pain the separation brings!

The pheasant, though no more in view,
  His cry, below, above, forth sends.
Alas! my princely lord, 'tis you—
  Your absence, that my bosom rends.

At sun and moon I sit and gaze,
  In converse with my troubled heart.
Far, far from me my husband stays!
  When will he come to heal its smart?

Ye princely men who with him mate,
  Say, mark ye not his virtuous way.
His rule is—covet nought, none hate;—
  How can his steps from goodness stray?

THE PLAINT OF A REJECTED WIFE

The east wind gently blows,
  With cloudy skies and rain.
'Twixt man and wife should ne'er be strife,
  But harmony obtain.
Radish and mustard plants
  Are used, though some be poor;
While my good name is free from blame,
  Don't thrust me from your door.

I go along the road,
  Slow, with reluctant heart.
Your escort lame to door but came,
  There glad from me to part.
Sow-thistle, bitter called,
  As shepherd's purse is sweet;
With your new mate you feast elate,
  As joyous brothers meet.

Part clear, the stream of King
 Is foul beside the Wei.
You feast elate with your new mate,
 And take no heed of me.
Loose mate, avoid my dam,
 Nor dare my basket move!
Person slighted, life all blighted,
 What can the future prove?

The water deep, in boat,
 Or raft-sustained, I'd go;
And where the stream did narrow seem,
 I dived or breasted through.
I labored to increase
 Our means, or great or small;
When 'mong friends near death did appear,
 On knees to help I'd crawl.

No cherishing you give,
 I'm hostile in your eyes.
As pedler's wares for which none cares,
 My virtues you despise.
When poverty was nigh,
 I strove our means to spare;
You, now rich grown, me scorn to own;
 To poison me compare.

The stores for winter piled
 Are all unprized in spring.
So now, elate with your new mate,
 Myself away you fling.
Your cool disdain for me
 A bitter anguish hath.
The early time, our love's sweet prime,
 In you wakes only wrath.

SOLDIERS OF WEI BEWAIL SEPARATION FROM THEIR FAMILIES

List to the thunder and roll of the drum!
  See how we spring and brandish the dart!
Some raise Ts'aou's walls; some do field work at home;
  But we to the southward lonely depart.

Our chief, Sun Tsze-chung, agreement has made,
  Our forces to join with Ch'in and with Sung.
When shall we back from this service be led?
  Our hearts are all sad, our courage unstrung.

Here we are halting, and there we delay;
  Anon we soon lose our high-mettled steeds.
The forest's gloom makes our steps go astray;
  Each thicket of trees our searching misleads.

For death as for life, at home or abroad,
  We pledged to our wives our faithfulest word.
Their hands clasped in ours, together we vowed,
  We'd live to old age in sweetest accord.

This march to the South can end but in ill;
  Oh! never shall we our wives again meet.
The word that we pledged we cannot fulfil;
  Us home returning they never will greet.

AN OFFICER TELLS OF HIS MEAN EMPLOYMENT

With mind indifferent, things I easy take;
In every dance I prompt appearance make:—
Then, when the sun is at his topmost height,
There, in the place that courts the public sight.

With figure large I in the courtyard dance,
And the duke smiles, when he beholds me prance.
A tiger's strength I have; the steeds swift bound;
The reins as ribbons in my hands are found.

See how I hold the flute in my left hand;
In right the pheasant's plume, waved like a wand;
With visage red, where rouge you think to trace,
While the duke pleased, sends down the cup of grace!

Hazel on hills; the *ling* in meadow damp;—
Each has its place, while I'm a slighted scamp.
My thoughts go back to th' early days of Chow,
And muse upon its chiefs, not equalled now.
  O noble chiefs, who then the West adorned,
  Would ye have thus neglected me and scorned?

AN OFFICER SETS FORTH HIS HARD LOT

My way leads forth by the gate on the north;
  My heart is full of woe.
I hav'n't a cent, begged, stolen, or lent,
  And friends forget me so.
    So let it be! 'tis Heaven's decree.
    What can I say—a poor fellow like me?

The King has his throne, sans sorrow or moan;
  On me fall all his cares,
And when I come home, resolved not to roam,
  Each one indignant stares.
    So let it be! 'tis Heaven's decree.
    What can I say—a poor fellow like me?

Each thing of the King, and the fate of the State,
  On me come more and more.
And when, sad and worn, I come back forlorn,
  They thrust me from the door.
      So let it be! 'tis Heaven's decree.
      What can I say—a poor fellow like me?

THE COMPLAINT OF A NEGLECTED WIFE

When the upper robe is green,
With a yellow lining seen,
There we have a certain token,
Right is wronged and order broken.
How can sorrow from my heart
In a case like this depart?

Color green the robe displays;
Lower garment yellow's blaze.
Thus it is that favorite mean
In the place of wife is seen.
Vain the conflict with my grief;
Memory denies relief.

Yes, 'twas you the green who dyed,
You who fed the favorite's pride.
Anger rises in my heart,
Pierces it as with a dart.
But on ancient rules lean I,
Lest to wrong my thoughts should fly.

Fine or coarse, if thin the dress,
Cold winds always cause distress.
Hard my lot, my sorrow deep,
But my thoughts in check I keep.

Ancient story brings to mind
Sufferers who were resigned.

[NOTE.—Yellow is one of the five "correct" colors of the Chinese, while green is one of the "intermediate" colors that are less esteemed. Here we have the yellow used merely as a lining to the green, or employed in the lower, or less honorable, part of the dress;—an inversion of propriety, and intimating how a favorite had usurped the place of the rightful wife and thrust her down.]

IN PRAISE OF A MAIDEN

O sweet maiden, so fair and retiring,
    At the corner I'm waiting for you;
And I'm scratching my head, and inquiring
    What on earth it were best I should do.

Oh! the maiden, so handsome and coy,
    For a pledge gave a slim rosy reed.
Than the reed is she brighter, my joy;
    On her loveliness how my thoughts feed!

In the pastures a *t'e* blade she sought,
    And she gave it, so elegant, rare.
Oh! the grass does not dwell in my thought,
    But the donor, more elegant, fair.

DISCONTENT

As when the north winds keenly blow,
And all around fast falls the snow,
The source of pain and suffering great,
So now it is in Wei's poor state.
Let us join hands and haste away,
    My friends and lovers all.

'Tis not a time will brook delay;
　　Things for prompt action call.

As when the north winds whistle shrill,
And drifting snows each hollow fill,
The source of pain and suffering great,
So now it is in Wei's poor state.
Let us join hands, and leave for aye,
　　My friends and lovers all,
'Tis not a time will brook delay;
　　Things for prompt action call.

We look for red, and foxes meet;
For black, and crows our vision greet.
The creatures, both of omen bad,
Well suit the state of Wei so sad.
Let us join hands and mount our cars,
　　My friends and lovers all.
No time remains for wordy jars;
　　Things for prompt action call.

CHWANG KEANG BEMOANS HER HUSBAND'S CRUELTY

Fierce is the wind and cold;
　　And such is he.
Smiling he looks, and bold
　　Speaks mockingly.
Scornful and lewd his words,
　　Haughty his smile.
Bound is my heart with cords
　　In sorrow's coil.

As cloud of dust wind-blown,
  Just such is he.
Ready he seems to own,
  And come to me.
But he comes not nor goes,
  Stands in his pride.
Long, long, with painful throes,
  Grieved I abide.

Strong blew the wind; the cloud
  Hastened away.
Soon dark again, the shroud
  Covers the day.
I wake, and sleep no more
  Visits my eyes.
His course I sad deplore,
  With heavy sighs.

Cloudy the sky, and dark;
  The thunders roll.
Such outward signs well mark
  My troubled soul.
I wake, and sleep no more
  Comes to give rest.
His course I sad deplore,
  In anguished breast.

[Selections from Books IV, V, and VI have been omitted.]

BOOK VII

The Odes of Ch'ing

THE PEOPLE'S ADMIRATION FOR DUKE WOO

The black robes well your form befit;
  When they are worn we'll make you new.
Now for your court! oh! there we'll sit,
  And watch how you your duties do.
    And when we to our homes repair,
    We'll send to you our richest fare,
    Such is the love to you we bear!

Those robes well with your virtue match;
  When they are worn we'll make you new.
Now for your court! There will we watch,
  Well pleased, how you your duties do.
    And when we to our homes repair,
    We'll send to you our richest fare,
    Such is the love to you we bear!

Those robes your character beseem;
  When they are worn we'll make you new.
Now for your court! oh! there we deem
  It pleasure great your form to view.
    And when we to our homes repair,
    We'll send to you our richest fare,
    Such is the love to you we bear!

A WIFE CONSOLED BY HER HUSBAND'S ARRIVAL

Cold is the wind, fast falls the rain,
　The cock aye shrilly crows.
But I have seen my lord again;—
　Now must my heart repose.

Whistles the wind, patters the rain,
　The cock's crow far resounds.
But I have seen my lord again,
　And healed are my heart's wounds.

All's dark amid the wind and rain,
　Ceaseless the cock's clear voice!
But I have seen my lord again;—
　Should not my heart rejoice?

IN PRAISE OF SOME LADY

There by his side in chariot rideth she,
As lovely flower of the hibiscus tree,
So fair her face; and when about they wheel,
Her girdle gems of *Ken* themselves reveal.
For beauty all the House of Këang have fame;
Its eldest daughter—she beseems her name.

There on the path, close by him, walketh she,
Bright as the blossom of hibiscus tree,
And fair her face; and when around they flit,
Her girdle gems a tinkling sound emit.
Among the Këang she has distinguished place,
For virtuous fame renowned, and peerless grace.

A MAN'S PRAISE OF HIS WIFE

My path forth from the east gate lay,
Where cloud-like moved the girls at play.
Numerous are they, as clouds so bright,
But not on them my heart's thoughts light.
Dressed in a thin white silk, with coiffure gray,
Is she, my wife, my joy in life's low way.

Forth by the covering wall's high tower,
I went, and saw, like rush in flower,
Each flaunting girl. Brilliant are they,
But not with them my heart's thoughts stay.
In thin white silk, with head-dress madder-dyed,
Is she, my sole delight, 'foretime my bride.

AN ENTREATY

Along the great highway,
    I hold you by the cuff.
O spurn me not, I pray,
    Nor break old friendship off.

Along the highway worn,
    I hold your hand in mine.
Do not as vile me scorn;
    Your love I can't resign.

A WOMAN SCORNING HER LOVER

O dear! that artful boy
    Refuses me a word!
But, Sir, I shall enjoy
    My food, though you're absurd!

O dear! that artful boy
My table will not share!
But, Sir, I shall enjoy
My rest, though you're not there!

A LADY MOURNS THE ABSENCE OF HER STUDENT LOVER

You student, with the collar blue,
Long pines my heart with anxious pain.
Although I do not go to you,
Why from all word do you refrain?

O you, with girdle strings of blue,
My thoughts to you forever roam!
Although I do not go to you,
Yet why to me should you not come?

How reckless you, how light and wild,
There by the tower upon the wall!
One day, from sight of you exiled,
As long as three long months I call.

BOOK VIII

The Odes of Ts'e

A WIFE URGING HER HUSBAND TO ACTION

His lady to the marquis says,
  "The cock has crowed; 'tis late.
Get up, my lord, and haste to court.
  'Tis full; for you they wait."
She did not hear the cock's shrill sound,
Only the blueflies buzzing round.

Again she wakes him with the words,
  "The east, my lord, is bright.
A crowded court your presence seeks;
  Get up and hail the light."
'Twas not the dawning light which shone,
But that which by the moon was thrown.

He sleeping still, once more she says,
  "The flies are buzzing loud.
To lie and dream here by your side
  Were pleasant, but the crowd
Of officers will soon retire;
Draw not on you and me their ire!"

171

THE FOLLY OF USELESS EFFORT

The weeds will but the ranker grow,
  If fields too large you seek to till.
To try to gain men far away
  With grief your toiling heart will fill.

If fields too large you seek to till,
  The weeds will only rise more strong.
To try to gain men far away
  Will but your heart's distress prolong.

Things grow the best when to themselves
  Left, and to nature's vigor rare.
How young and tender is the child,
  With his twin tufts of falling hair!
But when you him ere long behold,
  That child shall cap of manhood wear!

THE PRINCE OF LOO

A grand man is the prince of Loo,
  With person large and high.
Lofty his front and suited to
  The fine glance of his eye!
Swift are his feet. In archery
  What man with him can vie?
With all these goodly qualities,
  We see him and we sigh!

Renowned through all the land is he,
  The nephew of our lord.
With clear and lovely eyes, his grace

May not be told by word.
All day at target practice,
  He'll never miss the bird.
Such is the prince of Loo, and yet
  With grief for him we're stirred!

All grace and beauty he displays,
  High forehead and eyes bright.
And dancing choice! His arrows all
  The target hit aright.
Straight through they go, and every one
  Lights on the self-same spot.
Rebellion he could well withstand,
  And yet we mourn his lot!

BOOK IX

The Odes of Wei

ON THE MISGOVERNMENT OF THE STATE

A fruit, small as the garden peach,
    May still be used for food.
A State, though poor as ours, might thrive,
    If but its rule were good.
Our rule is bad, our State is sad,
    With mournful heart I grieve.
All can from instrument and voice
    My mood of mind perceive.
Who know me not, with scornful thought,
    Deem me a scholar proud.
"Those men are right," they fiercely say,
    "What mean your words so loud?"
Deep in my heart my sorrows lie,
    And none the cause may know.
How should they know who never try
    To learn whence comes our woe?

The garden jujube, although small,
    May still be used for food.
A State, though poor as ours, might thrive,
    If but its rule were good.
Our rule is bad, our State is sad,
    With mournful heart I grieve.
Methinks I'll wander through the land,

My misery to relieve.
Who know me not, with scornful thought,
    Deem that wild views I hold.
"Those men are right," they fiercely say,
    "What mean your words so bold?"
Deep in my heart my sorrows lie,
    And none the cause may know.
How can they know, who never try
    To learn whence comes our woe?

THE MEAN HUSBAND

Thin cloth of dolichos supplies the shoes,
    In which some have to brave the frost and cold.
A bride, when poor, her tender hands must use,
    Her dress to make, and the sharp needle hold.
This man is wealthy, yet he makes his bride
    Collars and waistbands for his robes provide.

Conscious of wealth, he moves with easy mien;
    Politely on the left he takes his place;
The ivory pin is at his girdle seen:—
    His dress and gait show gentlemanly grace.
Why do we brand him in our satire here?
    'Tis this—his niggard soul provokes the sneer.

A YOUNG SOLDIER ON SERVICE

To the top of that tree-clad hill I go,
    And towards my father I gaze,
Till with my mind's eye his form I espy,
    And my mind's ear hears how he says:—
"Alas for my son on service abroad!

He rests not from morning till eve.
May he careful be and come back to me!
  While he is away, how I grieve!"

To the top of that barren hill I climb,
  And towards my mother I gaze,
Till with my mind's eye her form I espy,
  And my mind's ear hears how she says:—
"Alas for my child on service abroad!
  He never in sleep shuts an eye.
May he careful be, and come back to me!
  In the wild may his body not lie!"

Up the lofty ridge I, toiling, ascend,
  And towards my brother I gaze,
Till with my mind's eye his form I espy,
  And my mind's ear hears how he says:—
"Alas! my young brother, serving abroad,
  All day with his comrades must roam.
May he careful be, and come back to me,
  And die not away from his home."

BOOK X

The Odes of T‛ang

The wild geese fly the bushy oaks around,
With clamor loud. *Suh-suh* their wings resound,
As for their feet poor resting-place is found.
The King's affairs admit of no delay.
Our millet still unsown, we haste away.
No food is left our parents to supply;
When we are gone, on whom can they rely?
O azure Heaven, that shinest there afar,
When shall our homes receive us from the war?

The wild geese on the bushy jujube-trees
Attempt to settle and are ill at ease;—
Suh-suh their wings go flapping in the breeze.
The King's affairs admit of no delay;
Our millet still unsown, we haste away.
How shall our parents their requirements get?
How in our absence shall their wants be met?
O azure Heaven, that shinest there afar,
When shall our homes receive us from the war?

The bushy mulberry-trees the geese in rows
Seek eager and to rest around them close—
With rustling loud, as disappointment grows.

177

The King's affairs admit of no delay;
To plant our rice and maize we cannot stay.
How shall our parents find their wonted food?
When we are gone, who will to them be good?
O azure Heaven, that shinest there afar,
When shall our homes receive us from the war?

LAMENT OF A BEREAVED PERSON

A russet pear-tree rises all alone,
But rich the growth of leaves upon it shown!
I walk alone, without one brother left,
And thus of natural aid am I bereft.
Plenty of people there are all around,
But none like my own father's sons are found.
Ye travellers, who forever hurry by,
Why on me turn the unsympathizing eye?
No brother lives with whom my cause to plead;—
Why not perform for me the helping deed?

A russet pear-tree rises all alone,
But rich with verdant foliage o'ergrown.
I walk alone, without one brother's care,
To whom I might, amid my straits repair.
Plenty of people there are all around,
But none like those of my own name are found.
Ye travellers, who forever hurry by,
Why on me turn the unsympathizing eye?
No brother lives with whom my cause to plead;—
Why not perform for me the helping deed?

THE DRAWBACKS OF POVERTY

On the left of the way, a russet pear-tree
Stands there all alone—a fit image of me.
There is that princely man! O that he would come,
And in my poor dwelling with me be at home!
In the core of my heart do I love him, but say,
Whence shall I procure him the wants of the day?

At the bend in the way a russet pear-tree
Stands there all alone—a fit image of me.
There is that princely man! O that he would come,
And rambling with me be himself here at home!
In the core of my heart I love him, but say,
Whence shall I procure him the wants of the day?

A WIFE MOURNS FOR HER HUSBAND

The dolichos grows and covers the thorn,
  O'er the waste is the dragon-plant creeping.
The man of my heart is away and I mourn—
  What home have I, lonely and weeping?

Covering the jujubes the dolichos grows,
  The graves many dragon-plants cover;
But where is the man on whose breast I'd repose?
  No home have I, having no lover!

Fair to see was the pillow of horn,
  And fair the bed-chamber's adorning;
But the man of my heart is not here, and I mourn
  All alone, and wait for the morning.

While the long days of summer pass over my head,
   And long winter nights leave their traces,
I'm alone! Till a hundred of years shall have fled,
   And then I shall meet his embraces.

Through the long winter nights I am burdened with fears,
   Through the long summer days I am lonely;
But when time shall have counted its hundreds of years
   I then shall be his—and his only!

BOOK XI

The Odes of Ts'in

CELEBRATING THE OPULENCE OF THE LORDS OF TS'IN

Our ruler to the hunt proceeds;
And black as iron are his steeds
That heed the charioteer's command,
Who holds the six reins in his hand.
His favorites follow to the chase,
Rejoicing in his special grace.

The season's males, alarmed, arise—
The season's males, of wondrous size.
Driven by the beaters, forth they spring,
Soon caught within the hunters' ring.
"Drive on their left," the ruler cries;
And to its mark his arrow flies.

The hunting done, northward he goes;
And in the park the driver shows
The horses' points, and his own skill
That rules and guides them at his will.
Light cars whose teams small bells display,
The long- and short-mouthed dogs convey.

181

A COMPLAINT

He lodged us in a spacious house,
　And plenteous was our fare.
But now at every frugal meal
　There's not a scrap to spare.
Alas! alas that this good man
Could not go on as he began!

A WIFE'S GRIEF BECAUSE OF HER HUSBAND'S ABSENCE

The falcon swiftly seeks the north,
And forest gloom that sent it forth.
Since I no more my husband see,
My heart from grief is never free.
O how is it, I long to know,
That he, my lord, forgets me so?

Bushy oaks on the mountain grow,
And six elms where the ground is low.
But I, my husband seen no more,
My sad and joyless fate deplore.
O how is it, I long to know,
That he, my lord, forgets me so?

The hills the bushy wild plums show,
And pear-trees grace the ground below.
But, with my husband from me gone,
As drunk with grief, I dwell alone.
Oh how is it, I long to know,
That he, my lord, forgets me so?

LAMENT FOR THREE BROTHERS

They flit about, the yellow birds,
And rest upon the jujubes find.
Who buried were in duke Muh's grave,
Alive to awful death consigned?

'Mong brothers three, who met that fate,
'Twas sad the first, Yen-seih to see.
He stood alone; a hundred men
Could show no other such as he.
When to the yawning grave he came,
Terror unnerved and shook his frame.

Why thus destroy our noblest men,
To thee we cry, O azure Heaven!
To save Yen-seih from death, we would
A hundred lives have freely given.

They flit about, the yellow birds,
And on the mulberry-trees rest find.
Who buried were in duke Muh's grave,
Alive to awful death consigned?

'Mong brothers three, who met that fate,
'Twas sad the next, Chung-hang to see.
When on him pressed a hundred men,
A match for all of them was he.
When to the yawning grave he came,
Terror unnerved and shook his frame.

Why thus destroy our noblest men,
To thee we cry, O azure Heaven!
To save Chung-hang from death, we would
A hundred lives have freely given.

They flit about, the yellow birds,
    And rest upon the thorn-trees find.
Who buried were in duke Muh's grave,
    Alive to awful death consigned?

'Mong brothers three, who met that fate,
    'Twas sad the third, K'ëen-foo, to see.
A hundred men in desperate fight
    Successfully withstand could he.
When to the yawning grave he came,
Terror unnerved and shook his frame.

Why thus destroy our noblest men,
    To thee we cry, O azure Heaven!
To save K'ëen-foo from death, we would
    A hundred lives have freely given.

[NOTE.—The incident related in this poem occurred in the year B.C.
620, when the duke of Muh died after playing an important part in the
affairs of Northwest China. Muh required the three officers here celebrated, to be buried with him, and according to the "Historical Records"
this barbarous practice began with duke Ching, Muh's predecessor. In all,
170 individuals were buried with Muh. The death of the last distinguished
man of the Ts'in dynasty, the Emperor I, was subsequently celebrated by
the entombment with him of all the inmates of his harem.]

IN PRAISE OF A RULER OF TS'IN

What trees grow on the Chung-nan hill?
    The white fir and the plum.
In fur of fox, 'neath 'broidered robe,
    Thither our prince is come.
His face glows with vermilion hue.
O may he prove a ruler true!

What find we on the Chung-nan hill?
    Deep nook and open glade.

Our prince shows there the double *Ke*
On lower robe displayed.
His pendant holds each tinkling gem,
Long life be his, and deathless fame!

THE GENEROUS NEPHEW

I escorted my uncle to Tsin,
  Till the Wei we crossed on the way.
    Then I gave as I left
    For his carriage a gift
  Four steeds, and each steed was a bay.

I escorted my uncle to Tsin,
  And I thought of him much in my heart.
    Pendant stones, and with them
    Of fine jasper a gem,
  I gave, and then saw him depart.

BOOK XII

The Odes of Ch'in

THE CONTENTMENT OF A POOR RECLUSE

My only door some pieces of crossed wood,
    Within it I can rest enjoy.
I drink the water wimpling from the spring;
    Nor hunger can my peace destroy.

Purged from ambition's aims I say, "For fish,
    We need not bream caught in the Ho;
Nor, to possess the sweets of love, require
    To Ts'e, to find a Keang, to go.

"The man contented with his lot, a meal
    Of fish without Ho carp can make;
Nor needs, to rest in his domestic joy,
    A Tsze of Sung as wife to take."

THE DISAPPOINTED LOVER

Where grow the willows near the eastern gate,
    And 'neath their leafy shade we could recline,
She said at evening she would me await,
    And brightly now I see the day-star shine!

Here where the willows near the eastern gate
  Grow, and their dense leaves make a shady gloom,
She said at evening she would me await.
  See now the morning star the sky illume!

A LOVE-SONG

The moon comes forth, bright in the sky;
A lovelier sight to draw my eye
    Is she, that lady fair.
She round my heart has fixed love's chain,
But all my longings are in vain.
    'Tis hard the grief to bear.

The moon comes forth, a splendid sight;
More winning far that lady bright,
    Object of my desire!
Deep-seated is my anxious grief;
In vain I seek to find relief,
    While glows the secret fire.

The rising moon shines mild and fair;
More bright is she, whose beauty rare
    My heart with longing fills.
With eager wish I pine in vain;
O for relief from constant pain,
    Which through my bosom thrills!

THE LAMENT OF A LOVER

There where its shores the marsh surround,
Rushes and lotus plants abound.
Their loveliness brings to my mind
The lovelier one that I would find.

In vain I try to ease the smart
Of wounded love that wrings my heart.
In waking thought and nightly dreams,
From every pore the water streams.

All round the marsh's shores are seen
Valerian flowers and rushes green.
But lovelier is that Beauty rare,
Handsome and large, and tall and fair.
I wish and long to call her mine,
Doomed with the longing still to pine.
Nor day nor night e'er brings relief;
My inmost heart is full of grief.

Around the marsh, in rich display,
Grow rush and lotus flowers, all gay.
But not with her do they compare,
So tall and large, majestic, fair.
Both day and night, I nothing speed;
Still clings to me the aching need.
On side, on back, on face, I lie,
But vain each change of posture try.

BOOK XIII

The Odes of Kwei

THE WISH OF AN UNHAPPY MAN

Where the grounds are wet and low,
There the trees of goat-peach grow,
With their branches small and smooth,
Glossy in their tender youth.
Joy it were to me, O tree,
Consciousness to want like thee.

Where the grounds are wet and low,
There the trees of goat-peach grow.
Soft and fragrant are their flowers,
Glossy from the vernal showers.
Joy it were to me, O tree,
Ties of home to want like thee.

Where the grounds are wet and low,
There the trees of goat-peach grow,
What delicious fruits they bear,
Glossy, soft, of beauty rare!
Joy it were to me, O tree,
Household cares to want like thee.

BOOK XIV

The Odes of Ts'aou

AGAINST FRIVOLOUS PURSUITS

Like splendid robes appear the wings
   Of the ephemeral fly;
And such the pomp of those great men,
   Which soon in death shall lie!
I grieve! Would they but come to me!
   To teach them I should try.

The wings of the ephemeral fly
   Are robes of colors gay;
And such the glory of those men,
   Soon crumbling to decay!
I grieve! Would they but rest with me,
   They'd learn a better way!

The ephemeral fly bursts from its hole,
   With gauzy wings like snow;
So quick the rise, so quick the fall,
   Of those great men we know!
I grieve! Would they but lodge with me,
   Forth they would wiser go.

BOOK XV

The Odes of Pin

THE DUKE OF CHOW TELLS OF HIS SOLDIERS

To the hills of the East we went,
    And long had we there to remain.
When the word of recall was sent,
    Thick and fast came the drizzling rain.
When told our return we should take,
    Our hearts in the West were and sore;
But there did they clothes for us make:—
    They knew our hard service was o'er.
On the mulberry grounds in our sight
    The large caterpillars were creeping;
Lonely and still we passed the night,
    All under our carriages sleeping.

To the hills of the East we went,
    And long had we there to remain.
When the word of recall was sent,
    Thick and fast came the drizzling rain.
The heavenly gourds rise to the eye,
    With their fruit hanging under the eave.
In our chambers the sow-bug we spy;
    Their webs on our doors spiders weave.
Our paddocks seem crowded with deer,
    With the glow-worm's light all about.
Such thoughts, while they filled us with fear,
    We tried, but in vain, to keep out.

To the hills of the East we went,
  And long had we there to remain.
When the word of recall was sent,
  Thick and fast came the drizzling rain.
On ant-hills screamed cranes with delight;
  In their rooms were our wives sighing sore.
Our homes they had swept and made tight:—
  All at once we arrived at the door.
The bitter gourds hanging are seen,
  From branches of chestnut-trees high.
Three years of toil away we had been,
  Since such a sight greeted the eye.

To the hills of the East we went,
  And long had we there to remain.
When the word of recall was sent,
  Thick and fast came the drizzling rain.
With its wings now here, and now there,
  Is the oriole sporting in flight.
Those brides to their husbands repair,
  Their steeds red and bay, flecked with white.
Each mother has fitted each sash;
  Their equipments are full and complete;
But fresh unions, whatever their dash,
  Can ne'er with reunions compete.

THERE IS A PROPER WAY FOR DOING EVERYTHING

In hewing an axe-shaft, how must you act?
  Another axe take, or you'll never succeed.
In taking a wife, be sure 'tis a fact,
  That with no go-between you never can speed.

In hewing an axe-shaft, hewing a shaft,
   For a copy you have the axe in your hand.
In choosing a wife, you follow the craft,
   And forthwith on the mats the feast-vessels stand.

PART II.—MINOR ODES OF THE KINGDOM

BOOK I

Decade of Luh Ming

A FESTEL ODE

With sounds of happiness the deer
  Browse on the celery of the meads.
A nobler feast is furnished here,
  With guests renowned for noble deeds.
The lutes are struck; the organ blows,
  Till all its tongues in movement heave.
Each basket loaded stands, and shows
  The precious gifts the guests receive.
They love me and my mind will teach,
How duty's highest aim to reach.

With sounds of happiness the deer
  The southern-wood crop in the meads,
What noble guests surround me here,
  Distinguished for their worthy deeds!
From them my people learn to fly
  Whate'er is mean; to chiefs they give
A model and a pattern high;—
  They show the life they ought to live.
Then fill their cups with spirits rare,
Till each the banquet's joy shall share.

With sounds of happiness the deer
　　The salsola crop in the fields.
What noble guests surround me here!
　　Each lute for them its music yields.
Sound, sound the lutes, or great or small,
　　The joy harmonious to prolong;—
And with my spirits rich crown all
　　The cups to cheer the festive throng.
Let each retire with gladdened heart,
In his own sphere to play his part.

A FESTAL ODE COMPLIMENTING AN OFFICER

On dashed my four steeds, without halt, without stay,
Though toilsome and winding from Chow was the way.
I wished to return—but the monarch's command
Forbade that his business be done with slack hand;
　　And my heart was with sadness oppressed.

On dashed my four steeds; I ne'er slackened the reins.
They snorted and panted—all white, with black manes.
I wished to return, but our sovereign's command
Forbade that his business be done with slack hand;—
　　And I dared not to pause or to rest.

Unresting the Filial doves speed in their flight,
Ascending, then sweeping swift down from the height,
Now grouped on the oaks. The king's high command
Forbade that his business be done with slack hand;—
　　And my father I left, sore distressed.

Unresting the Filial doves speed in their flight,
Now fanning the air and anon they alight
On the medlars thick grouped. But our monarch's command
　　mand

Forbade that his business be done with slack hand;—
   Of my mother I thought with sad breast.

My four steeds I harnessed, all white and black-maned,
Which straight on their way, fleet and emulous strained.
I wished to return; and now venture in song
The wish to express, and announce how I long
   For my mother my care to attest.

[Note.—Both Maou and Choo agree that this ode was composed in honor of the officer who narrates the story in it, although they say it was not written by the officer himself, but was put into his mouth, as it were, to express the sympathy of his entertainer with him, and the appreciation of his devotion to duty.]

THE VALUE OF FRIENDSHIP

The woodmen's blows responsive ring,
   As on the trees they fall;
And when the birds their sweet notes sing,
   They to each other call.
From the dark valley comes a bird,
   And seeks the lofty tree.
Ying goes its voice, and thus it cries,
   "Companion, come to me."
The bird, although a creature small,
   Upon its mate depends;
And shall we men, who rank o'er all,
   Not seek to have our friends?
All spirits love the friendly man,
   And hearken to his prayer.
What harmony and peace they can
   Bestow, his lot shall share.

Hoo-hoo the woodmen all unite
   To shout, as trees they fell.

They do their work with all their might;—
  What I have done I'll tell.
I've strained and made my spirits clear,
  The fatted lambs I've killed.
With friends who my own surname bear,
  My hall I've largely filled.
Some may be absent, casually,
  And leave a broken line;
But better this than absence by
  An oversight of mine.
My court I've sprinkled and swept clean,
  Viands in order set.
Eight dishes loaded stand with grain;
  There's store of fatted meat.
My mother's kith and kin I'm sure
  I've widely called by name.
That some be hindered better is
  Than I give cause for blame.

On the hill-side the trees they fell,
  All working with good-will.
I labor too, with equal zeal,
  And the host's part fulfil.
Spirits I've set in order meet,
  The dishes stand in rows.
The guests are here; no vacant seat
  A brother absent shows.
The loss of kindly feeling oft
  From slightest things shall grow,
Where all the fare is dry and spare,
  Resentments fierce may glow.
My store of spirits is well strained,
  If short prove the supply,
My messengers I straightway send,
  And what is needed buy.

I beat the drums, and in the dance
   Lead joyously the train.
Oh! good it is, when falls the chance
   The sparkling cup to drain.

THE RESPONSE TO A FESTAL ODE

Heaven shields and sets thee fast.
It round thee fair has cast
   Thy virtue pure.
Thus richest joy is thine;—
Increase of corn and wine,
And every gift divine,
   Abundant, sure.

Heaven shields and sets thee fast.
From it thou goodness hast;
   Right are thy ways.
Its choicest gifts 'twill pour,
That last for evermore,
Nor time exhaust the store
   Through endless days.

Heaven shields and sets thee fast,
Makes thine endeavor last
   And prosper well.
Like hills and mountains high,
Whose masses touch the sky;
Like streams aye surging by;
   Thine increase swell!

With rite and auspice fair,
Thine offerings thou dost bear,
   And son-like give,

The season's round from spring,
To olden duke and king,
Whose words to thee we bring:—
"Forever live."

The spirits of thy dead
Pour blessings on thy head,
    Unnumbered sweet.
Thy subjects, simple, good,
Enjoy their drink and food.
Our tribes of every blood
    Follow thy feet.

Like moons that wax in light;
Or suns that scale the height;
    Or ageless hill;
Nor change, nor autumn know;
As pine and cypress grow;
The sons that from thee flow
    Be lasting still!

AN ODE OF CONGRATULATION

The russet pear-tree stands there all alone;
How bright the growth of fruit upon it shown!
The King's affairs no stinting hands require,
And days prolonged still mock our fond desire.
But time has brought the tenth month of the year;
My woman's heart is torn with wound severe.
Surely my warrior lord might now appear!

The russet pear-tree stands there all alone;
How dense the leafy shade all o'er it thrown!
The King's affairs require no slackening hand,
And our sad hearts their feelings can't command.

The plants and trees in beauty shine; 'tis spring.
From off my heart its gloom I fain would fling.
This season well my warrior home may bring!

I climbed that northern hill, and medlars sought;
The spring nigh o'er, to ripeness they were brought.
"The King's affairs cannot be slackly done";—
'Tis thus our parents mourn their absent son.
But now his sandal car must broken be;
I seem his powerful steeds worn out to see.
Relief has gone! He can't be far from me!

Alas! they can't have marched; they don't arrive!
More hard it grows with my distress to strive.
The time is passed, and still he is not here!
My sorrows multiply; great is my fear.
But lo! by reeds and shell I have divined,
That he is near, they both assure my mind;—
Soon at my side my warrior I shall find!

AN ODE ON THE RETURN OF THE TROOPS

Forth from the city in our cars we drove,
   Until we halted at the pasture ground.
The general came, and there with ardor strove
   A note of zeal throughout the host to sound.
   "Direct from court I come, by orders bound
The march to hasten";—it was thus he spake.
   Then with the carriage-officers around,
He strictly charged them quick despatch to make:—
"Urgent the King's affairs, forthwith the field we take."

While there we stopped, the second corps appeared,
   And 'twixt us and the city took its place.

The guiding standard was on high upreared,
  Where twining snakes the tortoises embrace,
  While oxtails, crest-like, did the staff's top grace.
We watched the sheet unfolding grandly wave;
  Each flag around showed falcons on its face.
With anxious care looked on our leader brave;
Watchful the carriage-officers appeared and grave.

Nan Chung, our chief, had heard the royal call
  To go where inroad by Heen-yuns was made,
And 'cross the frontier build a barrier wall.
  Numerous his chariots, splendidly arrayed!
  The standards—this where dragons were displayed,
And that where snakes round tortoises were coiled—
  Terrific flew. "Northward our host," he said,
"Heaven's son sends forth to tame the Heen-yun wild."
Soon by this awful chief would all their tribes be foiled.

When first we took the field, and northward went,
  The millet was in flower;—a prospect sweet.
Now when our weary steps are homeward bent,
  The snow falls fast, the mire impedes our feet.
  Many the hardships we were called to meet,
Ere the King's orders we had all fulfilled.
  No rest we had; often our friends to greet
The longing came; but vain regrets we stilled;
By tablets stern our hearts with fresh resolve were thrilled.

"Incessant chirp the insects in the grass;
  All round about the nimble hoppers spring.
From them our thoughts quick to our husbands pass,
  Although those thoughts our hearts with anguish wring.
  Oh! could we see them, what relief 'twould bring!
Our hearts, rejoiced, at once would feel at rest."
  Thus did our wives, their case deploring, sing;

The while our leader farther on had pressed,
And smitten with his power the wild Jung of the west.

The spring days now are lengthening out their light;
The plants and trees are dressed in living green;
The orioles resting sing, or wing their flight;
Our wives amid the southern-wood are seen,
Which white they bring, to feed their silkworms keen.
Our host, returned, sweeps onwards to the hall,
Where chiefs are questioned, shown the captives mean
Nan Chung, majestic, draws the gaze of all,
Proud o'er the barbarous foe his victories to recall.

BOOK II

The Decade of Pih H'wa

AN ODE APPROPRIATE TO A FESTIVITY

The dew lies heavy all around,
Nor, till the sun shines, leaves the ground.
Far into night we feasting sit;
We drink, and none his place may quit.

The dew lies heavy, and its gems
Stud the luxuriant, grassy stems.
The happy night with wassail rings;
So feasted here the former kings.

The jujube and the willow-tree
All fretted with the dew we see.
Each guest's a prince of noble line,
In whom the virtues all combine.

The *t'ung* and *e* their fruits display,
Pendant from every graceful spray.
My guests are joyous and serene,
No haggard eye, no ruffled mien.

BOOK III

The Decade of T'ung Kung

CELEBRATING A HUNTING EXPEDITION

Our chariots were well-built and firm,
    Well-matched our steeds, and fleet and strong.
Four, sleek and large, each chariot drew,
    And eastward thus we drove along.

Our hunting cars were light and good,
    Each with its team of noble steeds.
Still further east we took the way
    To Foo-mere's grassy plains that leads.

Loud-voiced, the masters of the chase
    Arranged the huntsmen, high and low.
While banners streamed, and ox-tails flew,
    We sought the prey on distant Gaou.

Each with full team, the princes came,
    A lengthened train in bright array.
In gold-wrought slippers, knee-caps red,
    They looked as on an audience day.

Each right thumb wore the metal guard;
    On the left arm its shield was bound.
In unison the arrows flew;
    The game lay piled upon the ground.

The leaders of the tawny teams
  Sped on their course, direct and true.
The drivers perfect skill displayed;
  Like blow well aimed each arrow flew.

Neighing and pleased, the steeds returned;
  The bannered lines back slowly came.
No jostling rude disgraced the crowd;
  The king declined large share of game.

So did this famous hunt proceed!
  So free it was from clamorous sound!
Well does our King become his place,
  And high the deeds his reign have crowned!

THE KING'S ANXIETY FOR HIS MORNING LEVÉE

How goes the night? For heavy morning sleep
Ill suits the king who men would loyal keep.
The courtyard, ruddy with the torch's light,
Proclaims unspent the deepest hour of night.
Already near the gate my lords appear;
Their tinkling bells salute my wakeful ear.

How goes the night? I may not slumber on.
Although not yet the night is wholly gone,
The paling torch-light in the court below
Gives token that the hours swift-footed go.
Already at the gate my lords appear;
Their tinkling bells with measured sound draw near.

How goes the night? I may not slumber now.
The darkness smiles with morning on its brow.
The courtyard torch no more gives forth its ray,

But heralds with its smoke the coming day.
My princes pass the gate, and gather there;
I see their banners floating in the air.

MORAL LESSONS FROM NATURAL FACTS

All true words fly, as from yon reedy marsh
The crane rings o'er the wild its screaming harsh.
Vainly you try reason in chains to keep;—
Freely it moves as fish sweeps through the deep.
Hate follows love, as 'neath those sandal-trees
The withered leaves the eager searcher sees.
The hurtful ne'er without some good was born;—
The stones that mar the hill will grind the corn.

All true words spread, as from the marsh's eye
The crane's sonorous note ascends the sky.
Goodness throughout the widest sphere abides,
As fish round isle and through the ocean glides.
And lesser good near greater you shall see,
As grows the paper shrub 'neath sandal-tree.
And good emerges from what man condemns;—
Those stones that mar the hill will polish gems.

BOOK IV

The Decade of K'e-foo

ON THE COMPLETION OF A ROYAL PALACE

On yonder banks a palace, lo! upshoots,
    The tender blue of southern hill behind;
Firm-founded, like the bamboo's clamping roots;
    Its roof made pine-like, to a point defined.
Fraternal love here bears its precious fruits,
    And unfraternal schemes be ne'er designed!

Ancestral sway is his. The walls they rear,
    Five thousand cubits long; and south and west
The doors are placed. Here will the king appear,
    Here laugh, here talk, here sit him down and rest.

To mould the walls, the frames they firmly tie;
    The toiling builders beat the earth and lime.
The walls shall vermin, storm, and bird defy;—
    Fit dwelling is it for his lordly prime.

Grand is the hall the noble lord ascends;—
    In height, like human form most reverent, grand;
And straight, as flies the shaft when bow unbends;
    Its tints, like hues when pheasant's wings expand.

High pillars rise the level court around;
    The pleasant light the open chamber steeps;
And deep recesses, wide alcoves, are found,
    Where our good king in perfect quiet sleeps.

207

Laid is the bamboo mat on rush mat square;—
  Here shall he sleep, and, waking, say, "Divine
What dreams are good? For bear and grizzly bear,
  And snakes and cobras, haunt this couch of mine."

Then shall the chief diviner glad reply,
  "The bears foreshow that Heaven will send you sons.
The snakes and cobras daughters prophesy.
  These auguries are all auspicious ones.

"Sons shall be his—on couches lulled to rest.
  The little ones, enrobed, with sceptres play;
Their infant cries are loud as stern behest;
  Their knees the vermeil covers shall display.
As king hereafter one shall be addressed;
  The rest, our princes, all the States shall sway.

"And daughters also to him shall be born.
  They shall be placed upon the ground to sleep;
Their playthings tiles, their dress the simplest worn;
  Their part alike from good and ill to keep,
And ne'er their parents' hearts to cause to mourn;
  To cook the food, and spirit-malt to steep."

THE CONDITION OF KING SEUEN'S FLOCKS

Who dares to say your sheep are few?
  The flocks are all three hundred strong.
Who dares despise your cattle too?
  There ninety, black-lipped, press along.
Though horned the sheep, yet peaceful each appears;
The cattle come with moist and flapping ears.

These climb the heights, those drink the pool;
  Some lie at rest, while others roam.
With rain-coats, and thin splint hats cool,
  And bearing food, your herdsmen come.
In thirties, ranged by hues, the creatures stand;
Fit victims they will yield at your command.

Your herdsmen twigs and fagots bring,
  With prey of birds and beasts for food.
Your sheep, untouched by evil thing,
  Approach, their health and vigor good.
The herdsman's waving hand they all behold,
And docile come, and pass into the fold.

Your herdsmen dream;—fish take the place
  Of men; on banners falcons fly,
Displacing snakes and tortoises.
  The augur tells his prophecy:—
"The first betoken plenteous years; the change
Of banners shows of homes a widening range."

BOOK V

The Decade of Seaou Min

A EUNUCH COMPLAINS OF HIS FATE

A few fine lines, at random drawn,
Like the shell-pattern wrought in lawn
   To hasty glance will seem.
My trivial faults base slander's slime
Distorted into foulest crime,
   And men me worthless deem.

A few small points, pricked down on wood,
May be made out a picture good
   Of the bright Southern Sieve.
Who planned, and helped those slanderers vile,
My name with base lies to defile?
   Unpitied, here I grieve.

With babbling tongues you go about,
And only scheme how to make out
   The lies you scatter round.
Here me—Be careful what you say;
People ere long your words will weigh,
   And liars you'll be found.

Clever you are with changeful schemes!
How else could all your evil dreams
   And slanders work their way?
Men now believe you; by and by,
The truth found out, each vicious lie
   Will ill for ill repay.

The proud rejoice; the sufferer weeps.
O azure Heaven, from out thy deeps
   Why look in silence down?
Behold those proud men and rebuke;
With pity on the sufferers look,
   And on the evil frown.

Those slanderers I would gladly take,
With all who help their schemes to make,
   And to the tigers throw.
If wolves and tigers such should spare,
I'd hurl them 'midst the freezing air,
   Where the keen north winds blow.
And should the North compassion feel
I'd fling them to great Heaven, to deal
   On them its direst woe.

As on the sacred heights you dwell,
My place is in the willow dell,
   One is the other near.
Before you, officers, I spread
These lines by me, poor eunuch, made.
   Think not Mang-tsze severe.

AN OFFICER DEPLORES THE MISERY OF THE TIME

In the fourth month summer shines;
In the sixth the heat declines.
Nature thus grants men relief;
Tyranny gives only grief.
Were not my forefathers men?
Can my suffering 'scape their ken?

In the cold of autumn days
Each plant shrivels and decays.
Nature then is hard and stern;
Living things sad lessons learn.
Friends dispersed, all order gone,
Place of refuge have I none.

Winter days are wild and fierce;
Rapid gusts each crevice pierce.
Such is my unhappy lot,
Unbefriended and forgot!
Others all can happy be;
I from misery ne'er am free.

On the mountains are fine trees;
Chestnuts, plum-trees, there one sees.
All the year their forms they show;
Stately more and more they grow.
Noble turned to ravening thief!
What the cause? This stirs my grief.

Waters from that spring appear
Sometimes foul, and sometimes clear,
Changing oft as falls the rain,
Or the sky grows bright again.
New misfortunes every day
Still befall me, misery's prey.

Aid from mighty streams obtained,
Southern States are shaped and drained.
Thus the Keang and Han are thanked,
And as benefactors ranked.
Weary toil my vigor drains;
All unnoticed it remains!

Hawks and eagles mount the sky;
Sturgeons in deep waters lie.
Out of reach, they safely get,
Arrow fear not, nor the net.
Hiding-place for me there's none;
Here I stay, and make my moan.

Ferns upon the hills abound;
Ke and e in marshy ground.
Each can boast its proper place,
Where it grows for use or grace.
I can only sing the woe,
Which, ill-starred, I undergo.

ON THE ALIENATION OF A FRIEND

Gently and soft the east wind blows,
    And then there falls the pelting rain.
When anxious fears pressed round you close,
    Then linked together were we twain.
Now happy, and your mind at rest,
You turn and cast me from your breast.

Gently and soft the east wind blows,
    And then there comes the whirlwind wild.
When anxious fears pressed round you close,
    Your bosom held me as a child.

Now happy, and in peaceful state,
You throw me off and quite forget.

Gently and soft the east wind blows,
   Then round the rocky height it storms.
Each plant its leaves all dying shows;
   The trees display their withered forms.
My virtues great forgotten all,
You keep in mind my faults, though small.

BOOK VI

The Decade of Pih Shan

A PICTURE OF HUSBANDRY

Various the toils which fields so large demand!
We choose the seed; we take our tools in hand.
In winter for our work we thus prepare;
Then in the spring, bearing the sharpened 'share,
We to the acres go that south incline,
And to the earth the different seeds consign.
Soon, straight and large, upward each plant aspires;—
All happens as our noble lord desires.

The plants will ear; within their sheath confined,
The grains will harden, and be good in kind.
Nor darnel these, nor wolf's-tail grass infests;
From core and leaf we pick the insect pests,
And pick we those that eat the joints and roots:—
So do we guard from harm the growing fruits.
May the great Spirit, whom each farmer names,
Those insects take, and cast them to the flames!

The clouds o'erspread the sky in masses dense,
And gentle rain down to the earth dispense.
First may the public fields the blessing get,
And then with it our private fields we wet!
Patches of unripe grain the reaper leaves;
And here and there ungathered are the sheaves.

215

Handfuls besides we drop upon the ground,
And ears untouched in numbers lie around;—
These by the poor and widows shall be found.

When wives and children to the toilers come,
Bringing provisions from each separate home,
Our lord of long descent shall oft appear;
The Inspector also, glad the men to cheer.
They too shall thank the Spirits of the air,
With sacrifices pure for all their care;
Now red, now black, the victims that they slay,
As North or South the sacrifice they pay;
While millet bright the altars always show;—
And we shall thus still greater blessings know.

THE COMPLAINT OF AN OFFICER

O Heaven above, before whose light
Revealed is every deed and thought,
　　To thee I cry.
Hither on toilsome service brought,
In this wild K'ew I watch time's flight,
　　And sadly sigh.
The second month had just begun,
When from the east we took our way.
　　Through summer hot
We passed, and many a wintry day.
Summer again its course has run.
　　O bitter lot!
There are my compeers, gay at court,
While here the tears my face begrime.
　　I'd fain return—
But there is that dread net for crime!
The fear of it the wish cuts short.
　　In vain I burn!

Ere we the royal city left,
The sun and moon renewed the year.
    We marched in hope.
Now to its close this year is near.
Return deferred, of hope bereft,
    All mourn and mope.
My lonesome state haunts aye my breast,
While duties grow, and cares increase,
    Too hard to bear.
Toils that oppress me never cease;
Not for a moment dare I rest,
    Nigh to despair.
I think with fond regard of those,
Who in their posts at court remain,
    My friends of old.
Fain would I be with them again,
But fierce reproof return would cause.
    This post I hold.

When for the West I left my home,
The sun and moon both mildly shone,
    Our hearts to cheer.
We'd soon be back, our service done!
Alas! affairs more urgent come,
    And fix us here.
The year is hastening to expire.
We gather now the southern-wood,
    The beans we reap;—
That for its fragrance, these for food.
Such things that constant care require
    Me anxious keep.
Thinking of friends still at their posts,
I rise and pass the night outside,
    So vexed my mind.

But soon what changes may betide?
I here will stay, whate'er it costs,
    And be resigned.

My honored friends, O do not deem
Your rest which seems secure from ill
    Will ever last!
Your duties quietly fulfil,
And hold the upright in esteem,
    With friendship fast.
So shall the Spirits hear your cry,
You virtuous make, and good supply,
    In measure vast.

My honored friends, O do not deem
Repose that seems secure from ill
    Will lasting prove.
Your duties quietly fulfil,
And hold the upright in esteem,
    With earnest love.
So shall the Spirits hear your prayer,
And on you happiness confer,
    Your hopes above.

BOOK VII

Decade of Sung Hoo

THE REJOICINGS OF A BRIDEGROOM

With axle creaking, all on fire I went,
   To fetch my young and lovely bride.
No thirst or hunger pangs my bosom rent—
   I only longed to have her by my side.
I feast with her, whose virtue fame had told,
Nor need we friends our rapture to behold.

The long-tailed pheasants surest covert find,
   Amid the forest on the plain.
Here from my virtuous bride, of noble mind,
   And person tall, I wisdom gain.
I praise her while we feast, and to her say,
"The love I bear you ne'er will know decay.

"Poor we may be; spirits and viands fine
   My humble means will not afford.
But what we have, we'll taste and not repine;
   From us will come no grumbling word.
And though to you no virtue I can add,
Yet we will sing and dance, in spirit glad.

"I oft ascend that lofty ridge with toil,
   And hew large branches from the oaks;
Then of their leafy glory them I spoil,

219

And fagots form with vigorous strokes.
Returning tired, your matchless grace I see,
And my whole soul dissolves in ecstasy.

"To the high hills I looked, and urged each steed;
    The great road next was smooth and plain.
Up hill, o'er dale, I never slackened speed;
    Like lute-string sounded every rein.
I knew, my journey ended, I should come
To you, sweet bride, the comfort of my home."

AGAINST LISTENING TO SLANDERERS

Like the blueflies buzzing round,
    And on the fences lighting,
Are the sons of slander found,
    Who never cease their biting.
O thou happy, courteous king,
To the winds their slanders fling.

Buzzing round the blueflies hear,
    About the jujubes flocking!
So the slanderers appear,
    Whose calumnies are shocking.
By no law or order bound,
All the kingdom they confound.

How they buzz, those odious flies,
    Upon the hazels clust'ring!
And as odious are the lies
    Of those slanderers blust'ring.
Hatred stirred between us two
Shows the evil they can do.

BOOK VIII

The Decade of Too Jin Sze

IN PRAISE OF BY-GONE SIMPLICITY

In the old capital they stood,
  With yellow fox-furs plain,
Their manners all correct and good,
  Speech free from vulgar stain.
Could we go back to Chow's old days,
All would look up to them with praise.

In the old capital they wore
  T'ae hats and black caps small;
And ladies, who famed surnames bore,
  Their own thick hair let fall.
Such simple ways are seen no more,
And the changed manners I deplore.

Ear-rings, made of plainest gold,
  In the old days were worn.
Each lady of a noble line
  A Yin or Keih seemed born.
Such officers and ladies now
I see not and my sorrows grow.

With graceful sweep their girdles fell,
  Then in the days of old.
The ladies' side-hair, with a swell,

Like scorpion's tail, rose bold.
Such, if I saw them in these days,
I'd follow with admiring gaze.

So hung their girdles, not for show;—
    To their own length 'twas due.
'Twas not by art their hair curled so;—
    By nature so it grew.
I seek such manners now in vain,
And pine for them with longing pain.

[NOTE.—Yin and Keih were clan names of great families, the ladies of
which would be leaders of fashion in the capital.]

A WIFE BEMOANS HER HUSBAND'S ABSENCE

So full am I of anxious thought,
Though all the morn king-grass I've sought,
    To fill my arms I fail.
Like wisp all-tangled is my hair!
To wash it let me home repair.
    My lord soon may I hail!

Though 'mong the indigo I've wrought
The morning long; through anxious thought,
    My skirt's filled but in part.
Within five days he was to appear;
The sixth has come and he's not here.
    Oh! how this racks my heart!

When here we dwelt in union sweet,
If the hunt called his eager feet,
    His bow I cased for him.
Or if to fish he went away,
And would be absent all the day,
    His line I put in trim.

What in his angling did he catch?
Well worth the time it was to watch
  How bream and tench he took.
Men thronged upon the banks and gazed;
At bream and tench they looked amazed,
  The triumphs of his hook.

THE EARL OF SHAOU'S WORK

As the young millet, by the genial rain
  Enriched, shoots up luxuriant and tall,
So, when we southward marched with toil and pain,
  The Earl of Shaou cheered and inspired us all.

We pushed our barrows, and our burdens bore;
  We drove our wagons, and our oxen led.
"The work once done, our labor there is o'er,
  And home we travel," to ourselves we said.

Close kept our footmen round the chariot track;
  Our eager host in close battalions sped.
"When once our work is done, then we go back,
  Our labor over," to themselves they said.

Hard was the work we had at Seay to do,
  But Shaou's great earl the city soon upreared.
The host its service gave with ardor true;—
  Such power in all the earl's commands appeared!

We did on plains and low lands what was meet;
  We cleared the springs and streams, the land to drain.
The Earl of Shaou announced his work complete,
  And the King's heart reposed, at rest again.

THE PLAINT OF KING YEW'S FORSAKEN WIFE

The fibres of the white-flowered rush
  Are with the white grass bound.
So do the two together go,
  In closest union found.
And thus should man and wife abide,
  The twain combined in one;
But this bad man sends me away,
  And bids me dwell alone.

Both rush and grass from the bright clouds
  The genial dew partake.
Kind and impartial, nature's laws
  No odious difference make.
But providence appears unkind;
  Events are often hard.
This man, to principle untrue,
  Denies me his regard.

Northward the pools their waters send,
  To flood each paddy field;
So get the fields the sap they need,
  Their store of rice to yield.
But that great man no deed of grace
  Deigns to bestow on me.
My songs are sighs. At thought of him
  My heart aches wearily.

The mulberry branches they collect,
  And use their food to cook;
But I must use a furnace small,
  That pot nor pan will brook.

So me that great man badly treats,
  Nor uses as his wife,
Degrades me from my proper place,
  And fills with grief my life.

The bells and drums inside the court
  Men stand without and hear;
So should the feelings in my breast,
  To him distinct appear.
All-sorrowful, I think of him,
  Longing to move his love;
But he vouchsafes no kind response;
  His thoughts far from me rove.

The marabow stands on the dam,
  And to repletion feeds;
The crane deep in the forest cries,
  Nor finds the food it needs.
So in my room the concubine
  By the great man is placed;
While I with cruel banishment
  Am cast out and disgraced.

The yellow ducks sit on the dam,
  With left wing gathered low;
So on each other do they lean,
  And their attachment show.
And love should thus the man and wife
  In closest concord bind;
But that man turns away from me,
  And shows a fickle mind.

When one stands on a slab of stone,
  No higher than the ground,
Nothing is added to his height;—
  Low with the stone he's found.

So does the favorite's mean estate
    Render that great man mean,
While I by him, to distance sent,
    Am pierced with sorrow keen.

HOSPITALITY

A few gourd leaves that waved about
    Cut down and boiled;—the feast how spare!
But the good host his spirits takes,
    Pours out a cup, and proves them rare.

A single rabbit on the mat,
    Or baked, or roast:—how small the feast!
But the good host his spirits takes,
    And fills the cup of every guest.

A single rabbit on the mat,
    Roasted or broiled:—how poor the meal!
But the guests from the spirit vase
    Fill their host's cup, and drink his weal.

A single rabbit on the mat,
    Roasted or baked:—no feast we think!
But from the spirit vase they take,
    Both host and guests, and joyous drink.

ON THE MISERY OF SOLDIERS

Yellow now is all the grass;
All the days in marching pass.
On the move is every man;
Hard work, far and near, they plan.

Black is every plant become;
Every man is torn from home.
Kept on foot, our state is sad;—
As if we no feelings had!

Not rhinoceroses we!
Tigers do we care to be?
Fields like these so desolate
Are to us a hateful fate.

Long-tailed foxes pleased may hide
'Mong the grass, where they abide.
We, in box carts slowly borne,
On the great roads plod and mourn.

BOOK I

Decade of King Wan

CELEBRATING KING WAN

The royal Wan now rests on high,
Enshrined in brightness of the sky.
Chow as a state had long been known,
And Heaven's decree at last was shown.
Its lords had borne a glorious name;
God kinged them when the season came.
King Wan ruled well when earth he trod;
Now moves his spirit near to God.

A strong-willed, earnest king was Wan,
And still his fame rolls widening on.
The gifts that God bestowed on Chow
Belong to Wan's descendants now.
Heaven blesses still with gifts divine
The hundred scions of his line;
And all the officers of Chow
From age to age more lustrous grow.

More lustrous still from age to age,
All reverent plans their zeal engage;
And brilliant statesmen owe their birth
To this much-favored spot of earth.

They spring like products of the land—
The men by whom the realm doth stand.
Such aid their numerous bands supply,
That Wan rests tranquilly on high.

Deep were Wan's thoughts, sustained his ways;
His reverence lit its trembling rays.
Resistless came great Heaven's decree;
The sons of Shang must bend the knee;—
The sons of Shang, each one a king,
In numbers beyond numbering.
Yet as God spoke, so must it be:—
The sons of Shang all bent the knee.

Now each to Chow his homage pays—
So dark and changing are Heaven's ways.
When we pour our libations here,
The officers of Shang appear,
Quick and alert to give their aid:—
Such is the service by them paid,
While still they do not cast aside
The cap and broidered axe—their pride.
Ye servants of our line of kings,
Remember him from whom it springs.

Remember him from whom it springs;—
Let this give to your virtue wings.
Seek harmony with Heaven's great mind;—
So shall you surest blessing find.
Ere Shang had lost the nation's heart,
Its monarchs all with God had part
In sacrifice. From them you see
'Tis hard to keep high Heaven's decree.

'Tis hard to keep high Heaven's decree!
O sin not, or you cease to be.
To add true lustre to your name,
See Shang expire in Heaven's dread flame.
For Heaven's high dealings are profound,
And far transcend all sense and sound.
From Wan your pattern you must draw,
And all the States will own your law.

[Selections from Book II are omitted.]

BOOK III

Decade of Tang

Grand shone the Milky Way on high,
With brilliant span athwart the sky,
   Nor promise gave of rain.
King Seuen long gazed; then from him broke,
In anguished tones the words he spoke.
   Well might he thus complain!
"O Heaven, what crimes have we to own,
That death and ruin still come down?
Relentless famine fills our graves.
Pity the king who humbly craves!
   Our miseries never cease.
To every Spirit I have vowed;
The choicest victim's blood has flowed.
As offerings I have freely paid
My store of gems and purest jade.
   Hear me, and give release!

"The drought consumes us. As on wing
Its fervors fly, and torment bring.
With purest mind and ceaseless care
My sacrifices I prepare.
At thine own border altars, Heaven,
And in my father's fane, I've given
   What might relief have found.

231

What Powers above, below, have sway,
To all my precious gifts I pay,
    Then bury in the ground.
Yes, every Spirit has received
Due honor, and, still unrelieved,
    Our sufferings greater grow.
How-tseih can't give the needed aid,
And help from God is still delayed!
The country lies a ruined waste.
O would that I alone might taste
    This bitter cup of woe!

"The drought consumes us. Nor do I
To fix the blame on others try.
I quake with dread; the risk I feel,
As when I hear the thunders peal,
    Or fear its sudden crash.
Our black-haired race, a remnant now,
Will every one be swept from Chow,
    As by the lightning's flash.
Nor I myself will live alone.
God from his great and heavenly throne
    Will not spare even me.
O friends and officers, come, blend
Your prayers with mine; come, lowly bend.
Chow's dynasty will pass away;
Its altars at no distant day
    In ruins all shall be!

"The drought consumes us. It keeps on
Its fatal course. All hope is gone.
The air more fierce and fiery glows.
Where can I fly? Where seek repose?
    Death marks me for its prey.
Above, no saving hand! Around,

No hope, no comfort, can be found.
The dukes and ministers of old
Give us no help. Can ye withhold
Your sympathy, who lately reigned?
And parents, how are you restrained,
    In this so dreadful day?

"The drought consumes us. There on high
The hills are parched. The streams are dry.
Drought's demon stalks abroad in ire,
And scatters wide his flames and fire.
    Alas, my woful heart!
The fires within its strength consume;
The heat without creates a gloom
    That from it will not part.
The dukes and ministers by-gone
Respond not to my prayer and moan.
God in great Heaven, permission give
That I may in retirement live,
    And try to heal my smart!

"The drought consumes us. Still I strive,
And will not leave while I survive.
    Duty to shun I fear.
Why upon me has come this drought?
Vainly I try to search it out,
    Vainly, with quest severe.
For a good harvest soon I prayed,
Nor late the rites I duly paid,
To Spirits of the air and land.
There wanted nought they could demand,
    Their favor to secure.
God in great Heaven, be just, be kind!
Thou dost not bear me in Thy mind.

My cry, ye wisest Spirits, hear!
Ye whom I constantly revere,
    Why do I this endure?

"The drought consumes us. People fly,
And leave their homes. Each social tie
    And bond of rule is snapt.
The Heads of Boards are all perplexed;
My premier's mind is sorely vexed;
    In trouble all are wrapt.
The Masters of my Horse and Guards;
My cook, and men of different wards:—
Not one has from the struggle shrunk.
Though feeling weak, they have not sunk,
    But done their best to aid.
To the great sky I look with pain;—
Why do these grievous sorrows rain
    On my devoted head?

"Yes, at the mighty sky I gaze,
And lo! the stars pursue their maze,
    And sparkle clear and bright.
Ah! Heaven nor helps, nor seems to ken.
Great officers and noble men,
With all your powers ye well have striven,
And reverently have sought from Heaven
    Its aid in our great fight.
My death is near; but oh! keep on,
And do as thus far you have done.
    Regard you only me?
No, for yourselves and all your friends,
On whom for rule the land depends,
    You seek security.
I turn my gaze to the great sky;—
When shall this drought be done, and I
    Quiet and restful be?"

PART IV.— ODES OF THE TEMPLE AND ALTAR

BOOK I

Sacrificial Odes of Chow

APPROPRIATE TO A SACRIFICE TO KING WAN

My offerings here are given,
    A ram, a bull.
Accept them, mighty Heaven,
    All-bountiful.

Thy statutes, O great king,
    I keep, I love;
So on the realm to bring
    Peace from above.

From Wan comes blessing rich;
    Now on the right
He owns those gifts to which
    Him I invite.

Do I not night and day,
    Revere great Heaven,
That thus its favor may
    To Chow be given?

ON SACRIFICING TO THE KINGS WOO, CHING, AND K'ANG

The arm of Woo was full of might;
   None could his fire withstand;
And Ching and K'ang stood forth to sight,
   As kinged by God's own hand.

We err not when we call them sage.
   How grandly they maintained
Their hold of all the heritage
   That Wan and Woo had gained!

As here we worship, they descend,
   While bells and drums resound,
And stones and lutes their music blend.
   With blessings we are crowned.

The rites correctly we discharge;
   The feast we freely share.
Those Sires Chow's glory will enlarge,
   And ever for it care.

THE END